BRADLEY WIGGINS

MY STORY

www.**totallyrandombooks**.co.uk

BRADLEY WIGGINS

WITH WILLIAM FOTHERINGHAM

MY STORY

RED FOX

BRADLEY WIGGINS: MY STORY
A RED FOX BOOK 978 1 849 41934 5

First published in Great Britain as *Bradley Wiggins: My Time* by Yellow Jersey Press

Abridged children's edition published in Great Britain by Red Fox,
an imprint of Random House Children's Publishers UK
A Random House Group Company

Yellow Jersey edition published 2012
This edition published 2013

1 3 5 7 9 10 8 6 4 2

The Random House Group Limited supports the Forest Stewardship Council (FSC®), the leading
international forest-certification organisation. Our books carrying the FSC label are printed on
FSC®-certified paper. FSC is the only forest certification scheme supported by the leading
environmental organisations, including Greenpeace. Our paper procurement policy can
be found at www.randomhouse.co.uk/environment.

MIX
Paper from
responsible sources
FSC
www.fsc.org   FSC® C016897

Set in Bembo 14/18pt

Red Fox Books are published by Random House Children's Publishers UK,
61–63 Uxbridge Road, London W5 5SA

www.**randomhousechildrens**.co.uk
www.**totallyrandombooks**.co.uk
www.**randomhouse**.co.uk

Addresses for companies within The Random House Group Limited can be found at:
www.randomhouse.co.uk/offices.htm

THE RANDOM HOUSE GROUP Limited Reg. No. 954009

A CIP catalogue record for this book is available from the British Library.

Printed and bound by CPI Group (UK) Ltd, Croydon, CR0 4YY

FOR CATH, BEN, ISABELLA, MUM,
NAN, GEORGE AND RYAN

CONTENTS

FOREWORD by Robert Millar   ix

PROLOGUE   1
BRADLEY WIGGINS: PROFILE   8
1   From Herne Hill to Track Success   9
2   Onto the Road   21
3   Rock Bottom   30
4   Time for Truth   37
5   Back on Track   45
6   Breakthrough   63
7   Brothers in Arms   71
8   Tearing up Tradition   79
9   The Midas Touch   99
10 The Wingmen – and a Working-class Hero   114
11 Back in the Madhouse   125
12 In the Firing Line   144
13 The Other Team   151
14 Under Attack   161
15 Life in Yellow   169

16 Open Road   187

17 An Englishman in Paris   198

18 London Calling   211

19 The Rollercoaster   218

20 What Next?   230

ACKNOWLEDGEMENTS   239

APPENDIX I: A Cycling Glossary   241

APPENDIX II: The Golden Year   247

LIST OF ILLUSTRATIONS   251

FOREWORD

by Robert Millar

*Former professional cyclist, and winner of
the 'King of the Mountains' competition
in the 1984 Tour de France*

My first Tour de France was a muddle of feelings
and emotions, but I did have one moment of
clarity. I was hot, I was tired and my lower limbs
felt as if someone had filled them with lead. I
wasn't even certain where I was – all I knew was
that it was a village somewhere in south–central
France and there were about 60km to the finish
that day. My main focus for the last hour had
been a mosquito bite that had developed angrily
on my heel, just where shoe and foot met. It was
driving me crazy and I couldn't work out if it
actually hurt more than my legs.

It was a typical French village where you
could sense nothing much ever happened, but

because the Tour de France was passing through they were having a typical French village fête day to celebrate our arrival. The whole village had turned out to greet us and they were enjoying themselves just like the mosquito had. I felt annoyed.

And then, on the right-hand side, just as we left the houses and headed back into the trees, I noticed an old woman sitting on a chair outside her door. Dressed all in black, she must have been eighty if she was a day but she had a youthful twinkle in her eye and the world's biggest smile. I realized she was beaming with pride that we had come to her village. I knew then it was my duty not to disappoint her: I had to do my best, to be as good a Tour rider as I could be.

There's always a touch of theatre about each Tour de France; it may be a sporting competition but more often than not there's human drama each day. To be part of the show you already have to be good – very good. And to play one of the main roles you need every ounce of your talent, every last drop of your passion.

Over the following pages Bradley Wiggins

takes you through the trials and tribulations, through the tears and the training that have seen him transformed from mere contender to be a Tour de France champion.

What it took to be as good as he could be.

Robert Millar, November 2012

PROLOGUE

SATURDAY 21 JULY 2012
TOUR DE FRANCE

It is the last hour before the final **time trial**[†] of the **Tour de France**, and I am within reach of my open road. In every race, that's what I'm looking for: that sense of having clear space in front of me. That's when I feel truly in control. That open road can be the moment in a summit finish in the mountains where my last teammate peels off the group and it's all down to me; it can be the point where the strongmen in a stage race emerge and the fighting for position stops; or the moment when I have to come out of the jostling pack, and ramp the pace up so that my teammate Mark Cavendish can nail a finish sprint. That's where the physical

[†]For bold words, see glossary.

1

side takes over and all I have to do is turn the taps on full.

The routine for today is the same one I've built and perfected over fifteen years, and it is all timed to the second.

It counts back from the warm-up. In my head the warm-up – so essential for any athlete – is when my race starts: the moment when I leave the bus and get on the **turbo trainer** at *precisely* the right second.

The warm-up starts *exactly* half an hour before I go down the ramp to the start; so if my start time is three minutes past three, I'll get on the trainer at two thirty-three on the dot.

I like to get to the bus early, soak up the atmosphere, chat with the mechanics, make sure everything's OK with the bikes, and go through everything I need to know with my trainer.

We also:

- get taped up by the physios using **kinesio tape**; it's like putting on your armour before going into battle!
- do a bit of stretching in the back of the bus
- get the numbers on the suit and get changed

- smear on the chammy cream (anti–chafing)
- Then leave the suit unzipped and put a vest on.

Every now and then little demons appear in my head. Something in my mind says:

What if you puncture?

What if the chain snaps?

What if I lose two minutes?

Silly little things like that. I try to put these worries to bed, but it's a constant background noise. I've stopped thinking rationally.

Thirty minutes to warm-up

I start listening to my playlist. It's a dance-music mix that a former teammate did for me a couple of years ago. I always start listening to it at exactly the same time; any earlier and I begin getting into the zone too soon.

Twenty minutes to warm-up

Shoes on.

Ten minutes to warm-up

Lace shoes up.

Zero hour – warm-up

Out of the bus and onto the turbo. Screens tick over the minutes in front of the turbo trainers, where the team staff set up fans to cool us down and bottles of energy drinks. There are also clocks – the first thing the staff do, as soon as they arrive at the start area in the morning, is to sync all the clocks with the start clock on the ramp. There's no point in timing your warm-up using your watch. It might be five minutes fast, in which case you'd arrive at the start with eight minutes to go instead of three and be sitting around for too long; worst of all, if your watch is slow, you'd get there late.

My warm-up takes exactly twenty minutes. I've done it for fifteen years, the same ramping up in power. I push myself up to **threshold** and then I'm totally in my own world.

I am in the zone.

As I turn the pedals on the turbo trainer, people pass by but I see no one. Most of the time my eyes are closed. I'm going through the ride in my head: sitting on the start ramp, flying down off it. I'm constantly sensing what it's going to feel like, imagining lying on the time-trial handlebars, or **skis**, as we call them.

In my head it's feeling strong, flowing, everything's working. It's easy, I'm floating along, I'm gliding, it's feeling great.

Ten minutes to start
Off the turbo.
Into the bus.
Go to the loo.
Overshoes on, gloves on.
Wipe down.
Sit down for a couple of minutes.
Calm down.

Six minutes to start
My trainer comes in. 'Let's go.'
Clip on visor.
Go down towards the cordoned-off area around the ramp.
Find a chair straight away and keep going through the start process in my head.
Try to get away from the photographers' flashbulbs.
Vincenzo Nibali, who is third overall, is just starting . . .

Three minutes to start

My teammate Chris Froome – second overall – comes down the ramp and I go up the steps. I'm looking at him in the distance and the car following him, and as they get further and further out of sight my mind gets really positive, really aggressive: I'm coming after you, I'll be seeing that soon – that kind of feeling.

Chris is my teammate but there are no teammates in time trialling: it's you against the clock and you against everybody else. In this race, on this specific day, Chris is like the rest of them – and he is my closest competitor.

And I am going after him.

One minute to start

Clip into the pedals.

Go to the starter.

I want to nail it.

Five seconds

Throw the body back on the bike; push back onto the guy holding the saddle as if my back wheel is locked into a start gate on the track.

Three
Deep breath in. Fill the lungs.

Two
Deep breath out.

One
Breathe in, deep as I can.

Winning the Tour de France is one good ride
away . . .

BRADLEY WIGGINS

BORN 28 April 1980, Ghent, Belgium

STAR SIGN Taurus

FATHER Gary Wiggins, professional cyclist; Australian

MOTHER Linda, school secretary; English

LIVED London, from 1982. Now lives in Lancashire

FAMILY Married to Catherine; they have two children

NICKNAME Wiggo

HEIGHT 1.90m (6ft 3in)

WEIGHT 69kg (150lb; 10.9st), though closer to 78kg in his track days

CURRENT BIKE A Pinarello Graal (Sky Team)

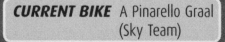

FROM HERNE HILL TO TRACK SUCCESS

My career began in **track cycling**. As a twelve-year-old, I used to race at south London's Herne Hill Velodrome, and I was chosen to represent Camden in the London Youth Games as a teenager.

I followed cycling with a passion. And although I was a track cyclist, I always knew somehow that – for me – the greatest race in the world would always be the Tour de France. I've always been into it, since I was a teenager watching videos of the race rather than doing my homework.

At thirteen, with my mum, I went to Paris and watched the riders coming up the Champs-

Élysées on the final stage of the race. We'd come over from London for the weekend, gone up the Eiffel Tower on the Saturday, then come to see the Tour on the Sunday.

It was my first sight of the Tour. I'm standing on the railings just before the kilometre-to-go kite on the entrance to the square, with my mother and my brother, watching them all go past. It's 25 July 1993; I remember spotting Miguel Indurain in the **yellow jersey**, Gianni Bugno in the rainbow jersey of world champion.

I was hooked, but I never imagined that nineteen years later I'd be coming down there in the same position!

Cycling wasn't my only love. I've always been gripped by music and a song will always take me back to when I first heard it. The one I remember as being the first to really amaze me was *Don't Stop* by the Stone Roses. I was only eleven, but I really started getting into their music. And then I saw The Smiths on *Top of the Pops 2*, when I was round my nan's one day. It wasn't the music that got me: it was the image of the guitarist – he looked so cool!

I guess my favourite all-time bands are probably The Jam, Oasis, Ocean Colour Scene, The Who and Small Faces. Oh, and I really love Paul Weller's music . . .

DID YOU KNOW?

Brad has over a dozen guitars!

I first met Shane Sutton — one of the key men behind my success nowadays — when I was still a schoolboy. At the 1996 national track championships, aged sixteen, I had finished third in the junior points race, and after I'd come down off the podium, he was crouched there and chatting away, telling me how he had raced with my dad, Gary Wiggins, in Australia. I don't think they got on very well, though — Shane was a tough little nut and so was my dad, so they never saw eye to eye.

I also met Sean Yates — now the *directeur sportif* at Sky — way back as a teenager. In 1997, at fifteen, I made the trip to the British Cycling Federation dinner during the off-season, to be presented with the trophy for the juvenile points race. It was Sean who was handing out the prizes — many years later I still had the photo of

SEAN YATES

Having the fastest time at the sixth stage in 1994, Sean Yates is one of only four people from the UK to have ever worn the yellow jersey in the Tour de France (the others were Tom Simpson, Chris Boardman and David Millar). In 1988, Yates set a new Tour de France record speed at the Wasquehal time trial. In 2010, Yates became manager of Team Sky and worked closely with Bradley Wiggins up to his Tour de France victory in 2012.

us together at the dinner, and just before the Tour de France of 2012, I made a point of sending Sean that picture and I said to him, 'I bet you never thought that kid would become a contender one day!'

Sean and I share a lot of history. He was one of my heroes as a kid – and at the Tour of Flanders in 1996, when I was just fourteen, I went up to him at the start and asked him for his autograph. Back then, Robert Millar, Chris Boardman and Sean Yates were the Brits in the professional **peloton**, and for various reasons Sean was the fans' choice. He wasn't a big winner, although he won a lot of decent races and wore the yellow jersey for a day in the Tour in 1994, but within the cycling world we loved Sean – he was someone who came from our world of club cycling and winter runs.

Sean's last season as a full-on professional was 1996, but he made a comeback in 1998 to ride the Tour of Britain for the Linda McCartney team – sponsored by the vegetarian food company owned by the late wife of the former Beatle.

I was the junior world pursuit champion by then and was racing at Herne Hill in the **team pursuit**. The teams were a mix of young riders and stars of the past and I was in Sean's team. I remember he said to me afterwards, 'I was really struggling to hold your wheel.' He was lovely. He wasn't behaving like a lot of old pros when you're that age, who seem to be trying to put you down a bit: 'Don't get too big for your boots, this means nothing in the juniors, you've still got to break through.' He was really praising me: 'You're going to be really good one day.' And I was thinking, 'This is Sean Yates telling me this.' I remember it really sinking in: Sean Yates said to me I'm going to be really good one day!

At the end of 1998 after I won the Junior World's, he asked me if I would like to join McCartney for '99. I said no, I'd love to, thanks, but I was going to stay with British Cycling. By 2000 McCartney had grown, and I heard that Sean wanted to ask me to join, but he didn't because he knew I was on the Olympic squad and wanted to ride the team pursuit in Sydney. After the Olympics that summer, where I got a bronze medal in the team pursuit, he rang me at my mum's.

'Right: do you want to go pro with us next year? We can pay you thirty-five grand.' And that was that.

I signed; then, at the age of twenty-one, I loaded my Fiesta up and drove to their base in Toulouse. I had to drive down there with only one wing mirror because someone had smashed the other one off when it was parked in London, but it didn't matter because the front passenger seat was full of stuff anyway!

Sadly, it all came unstuck – the expected sponsorship hadn't come through, and the team was dead in the water. Luckily, the GB squad took me back, and in 2002 Shane Sutton came on board at British Cycling to help us with the

Madison – the two-man relay race in which I'd got close to a medal at the Sydney Olympics. We were always struggling to qualify teams for the World Track Championships in that event, so I saw more of him as we trained.

Early six-day cycle races were exhausting for the riders – spectators loved them, but riders frequently fell and 'their faces became hideous with the tortures that rack them' (*New York Times*, in 1897). Laws were passed in New York, USA, that ruled that no competitor could race for more than twelve hours. The promoter at Madison Square Gardens then designed a race in which each rider got a partner – the Madison – so he could keep his stadium open 24 hours a day!

After the Commonwealth Games that year Cath – now my wife – and I really got together properly. We'd met years before when we were both on the junior track squad, but now I went to live with her in Manchester, where she was at university and still riding the track. Cath understands the cycling world totally – her family have been in the sport for fifty years, and her father works at British Cycling.

I spent 2002 mostly racing with the French team Française des Jeux, while Cath was at university all day. That winter, I rode some of the German Six-Day races, on the tracks at Dortmund and Munich, and Shane came with me as my mechanic. We had a massive laugh (plus a few sessions sinking beers). I was only twenty-two, and didn't really understand yet how much you needed to work to get to the very top – what hard training is, and how much of a lifestyle change is involved. Much less drinking, for a start!

When Simon Jones, my coach since 1998, left British Cycling in early 2007, Shane was brought in to oversee the team pursuit squad. He had been working with British Cycling already, but not on the endurance squad of which I was a part; he was quite heavily involved with the team **sprinters**, like Chris Hoy.

Shane's first words were, 'You've got to start getting some enjoyment back into this programme.' He asked me to lead the group. And then he said, 'We need to start loving our athletes a bit more.'

'What do you mean?'

'What do you need?'

He bought me a phone and a SIM card, and said, 'See this? This is the backbone. If you ever need anything, just ring me.'

He made me feel like a million dollars. And he was true to his word too. If I did need something, Shane would be the first person I would call.

Two golds at the Olympics

2007 and 2008 were very successful years for me on the track, culminating in two golds at the Olympic Games in Beijing – and a world record as part of the 4,000m Team Pursuit squad.

After the 2008 Olympics in Beijing – a terrific Olympics for the Great Britain team, who topped the cycling medal table with fourteen cycling medals in total: eight gold, four silver and two bronze – I made the momentous decision to focus on road racing.

My only goal for the previous four years had been to win at the Olympics – and now I had two gold medals. With that in the bag, by the end of 2008, I'd had enough of track racing and now I wanted to compete hard on the road . . .

TRACK CYCLING

Races are held in **velodromes**, on tracks built specially for cycling. A new velodrome was built in London for the 2012 Olympics.

There are two main categories of races: sprints, and endurance races. Most sprinters don't compete in endurance races, and vice versa.

Sprint races usually only cover about 8-10 laps of the track. They can be individual races, team, time trial or keirin (where riders follow a pacer on a moped or similar for a number of laps, and then sprint for the finish).

Endurance races are held over longer distances – as many as 200 laps for some races! These were Brad's endurance events: individual pursuit, team pursuit and the Madison (a team event where riders take turns to ride stages of the race).

The bikes can be a key factor in success or failure; they are specially made to be light and as aerodynamic as possible. Different styles of handlebars can be used for different events.

Team GB won nine medals in track cycling at the 2012 Olympics in London – seven gold, one silver and one bronze.

A TYPICAL TRACK BIKE

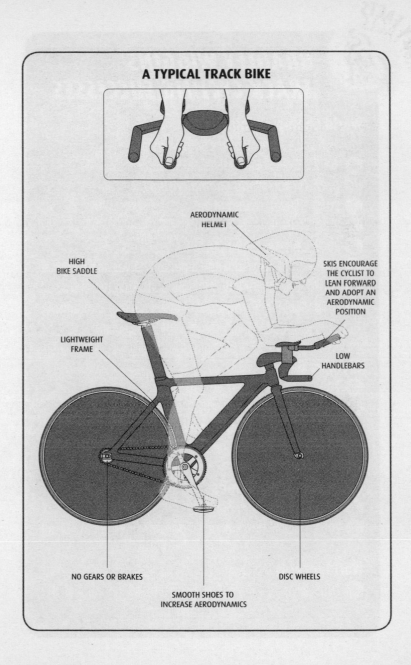

AERODYNAMIC HELMET

HIGH BIKE SADDLE

SKIS ENCOURAGE THE CYCLIST TO LEAN FORWARD AND ADOPT AN AERODYNAMIC POSITION

LIGHTWEIGHT FRAME

LOW HANDLEBARS

NO GEARS OR BRAKES

SMOOTH SHOES TO INCREASE AERODYNAMICS

DISC WHEELS

BRADLEY WIGGINS' TRACK CYCLING SUCCESSES

World Championships

Junior Track Cycling World Championships

- 1997 – Gold, 2km individual pursuit

UCI Track Cycling World Championships

- 2000 – Silver, team pursuit
- 2001 – Silver, team pursuit
- 2002 – Bronze, team pursuit
- 2003 – Gold, 4km individual pursuit; Silver, team pursuit
- 2007 – Gold, 4km individual pursuit; Gold, team pursuit
- 2008 – Gold, 4km individual pursuit; Gold, team pursuit; Gold, Madison (with Mark Cavendish)

Olympic Games

- 2000 – Bronze, team pursuit
- 2004 – Gold, 4km individual pursuit; Silver, team pursuit; Bronze, Madison
- 2008 – Gold, 4km individual pursuit; Gold, team pursuit

Commonwealth Games

- 1998 – Silver, team pursuit
- 2002 – Silver, 4km individual pursuit; Silver, team pursuit

World records

- 2008 Olympics – 4000m Team Pursuit (as part of the Great Britain team)

ONTO THE ROAD

My first big success in road racing – **stage racing** – was in the summer of 2009.

I had signed with the American team Garmin in 2008, and my main goal was merely to earn a place in Garmin's squad for the Tour de France – the world's greatest bike race. To be there in the mountains, working for their team leader.

Garmin felt I had potential and offered me a good deal. So in 2009, I was loving riding my bike again. I was in a great set-up where it was a lot of fun, and we went out and got the job done.

ROAD CYCLING TEAMS

A cycling team is a group of cyclists who train and compete together in road cycle races, where team members must work together to get the best result for the team.

The leader of the team has the best chance of individual success as the rest of the team must work to support them. Bradley Wiggins was named as the leader of the Sky team when he signed with them.

A team will include members with different strengths. It would normally include, among others: **climbing specialists**, who can get up mountains; **sprinters**, who save their energy for last-minute sprint finishes; **time triallists**, who can keep a high speed up over a long distance; and **domestiques**, who keep the key members guarded from rival riders and carry the necessary water and food any team needs on a long ride.

To win the Tour de France, a team will need every single type of specialist.

Teams are sponsored; for instance, by bike manufacturers – so one team will use one kind of bicycle and another team a different make.

The very best teams belong to the **UCI World Tour**, which records all the results from a number of annual events and ranks riders according to their performances.

The 'big three' road cycling events – the ones every cyclist wants to win – are the three that take place over a number of days with different stages: the **Tour de France**, the **Giro d'Italia** (in Italy) and the **Vuelta a España** (Spain).

A TYPICAL ROAD BIKE

STANDARD
HELMET

HANDLEBARS ALLOW
DIFFERENT POSITIONS

GEARS AND
BRAKES

STRONG AND
LIGHTWEIGHT
FRAME

WATER BOTTLE

SPECIAL SHOES CAN
DRAIN RAINWATER

A great ride at the Tour de France

I went to the 2009 Tour feeling good, and several kilos lighter than I ever had been – an old GB track teammate had just had a pretty good year on the road after dropping his weight, so I thought I would try and do the same and see how it affected my performance, although I was of course having to eat a healthy, balanced diet. I was hoping I might even get into the top ten if everything went well.

The Tour went almost perfectly – I never had a bad day, did better than everyone had expected in the mountains and finally rode into Paris having finished fourth, the best British performance since Robert Millar managed the same placing in 1984.

I was completely on cloud nine. I had equalled the British record in the world's greatest bike race!

And now a new Pro team was interested in me . . .

Moving to Sky

Sky was a new team being formed for 2010 by Dave Brailsford, the performance director at British Cycling, and Shane, now their head coach – and they were on the hunt for a British rider who could challenge at the Tour. Their goal was to win the Tour with a British team within five years – and doing it clean (no riders with any history of **doping**).

My ride in 2009 came at the perfect time, and when Dave came to talk to me, I was sold straight away. I loved being with Garmin – they had believed in me and had given me the chance to do something on the road – but I'm a patriotic bloke, and the chance to lead a British team in the Tour was only going to come along once. The urge to go home was too strong.

After a lot of negotiations, the deal was finally done but from the end of the Tour in July until I signed with Sky in December – almost five months – I didn't have a team. And in all that time I hadn't really started training for this big race in France that we were going to try and win. I didn't even have a proper bike to train on: I was riding around on a bike made by an old mate in Lancashire. Garmin had taken back all the Felt bikes I had been riding for them, but until the deal with Sky was finalized, I hadn't been given a Pinarello to ride – the bike they used. So I hadn't started training.

The hype around the team was immense, and straight after the team launch in January 2010, we flew to Valencia for the first training camp. I was really unfit, and struggled for the first few days, but all the cameras were there and only one question was being asked: can you win the Tour within five years? But I still hadn't sat down with anyone for a phased planning session that answered the basic question: *Right, how are we going to do this?*

The 2010 Tour – my first for Sky
The Tour de France is a multiple-stage race that has 21 days of racing over a three-week period and covers 3,200 kilometres – that's 2,000 miles!

There are two rest days and the race always has at least two time-trial stages, a route that includes going through the mountain chains of

THE ROUTE

The route of the Tour de France changes every year, but the race must include flat, hilly, mountain and high-altitude stages. Since 1975 the finish has been on the Champs-Élysées in Paris.

the Pyrenees and the Alps and a finish in Paris.

The pressure on our team during the Tour that year was *massive*. I had finished fourth the year before so the natural assumption was also that I would perform better than before.

But the planner's dream went very wrong . . .

The **prologue** – the first day – was a nightmare. I wouldn't normally expect to finish 77th, even though I was riding in the rain!

There was a nasty crash on day two.

I got through that, and moved up to fourteenth overall, so coming towards the Alps at the end of the first week I was feeling good. I was beginning to think I might be OK, even on the first big Alpine climb. But by the time we got to the finish that day I knew it wasn't going to happen. As I crossed the line, a journalist asked me if that was the end of my Tour. I told him where to go!

DID YOU KNOW?

The Tour de France first began to help sell papers! In 1902 a new sports paper, *L'Auto,* was not selling well in France. To help promote the paper, a 26-year-old cycling journalist, Géo Lefèvre, suggested hosting the longest cycle race ever attempted. The first race was announced in January 1903.

I tried to fight on for the rest of the Tour, but it's hard to fight when you haven't got any form, because ultimately it depends on what strength you have in your legs. And I just hadn't been ready – hadn't done the training right, hadn't built up to this event properly. Every mountain day became a grind now as I wasn't quite good enough to stay with the first group when the racing got serious. I did have a couple of decent days – I was in the break one day in the Pyrenees and got a ninth in the last time trial – but it didn't count for anything.

I finished 24th, which shows that I was fit – what I was lacking was the last ten per cent that it takes to compete with the best guys. And it was massively disappointing after my fourth the previous year.

At the end of the Tour, all you want to do is get home. I didn't ride my bike for a week and then the Sunday after the Tour de France finished, I took part in the Manchester Sky Ride, one of a series of mass-participation cycle rides where thousands of members of the public could get on their bikes and pedal along with the stars.

That night I was sitting at home when my phone rang. It was my mum and she said, 'George has had a heart attack.'

George was my grandad.

ROCK BOTTOM

George had always been there. He was the father figure, the role model in my young life, from the day when my mother Linda and I moved into my nan and grandad's flat in Kilburn after my father Gary had walked out on us. For a while, until Mum got a small place of her own, I ended up living in a family which was mostly women: Nan and Grandad, and their three daughters – including my mum – and me.

I guess as I got older George was incredibly proud of me, but he never showed it. Even now, that side of my family doesn't hold me up as anything special – I'm just like any other cousin or grandchild. They don't really say, 'I'm so proud of you.' They'll still put me down or whatever – 'What've you got your hair like that for?' – which helps you keep a sense of who you are.

My father, Gary, was a hard-drinking Australian bike racer who had come over to Belgium to make a living competing on the track circuit there. I wasn't even two years old when he left – and he didn't so much walk out on us at Christmas 1982 as throw us out. We'd gone from our home in Ghent to see my mum's parents in London, and he just called my mum to say she and I weren't to come back to Belgium – he'd got together with someone else! He turned up later with four black bin liners containing our stuff from Belgium and dumped them at the bottom of the stairs to the flat where Nan and Grandad lived.

Gary moved to Australia later, but despite spending a little time together briefly, when I was in my late teens, we never built a proper relationship. He died over there in 2008, aged only 55.

I spent a lot of time with George for my first eight or nine years, so he was the man I thought of as being like a father; he brought me up.

And now he was in hospital – on life support.

Nine days later, the doctors told us they were going to turn the machines off. George's brain had been deprived of oxygen, so even if he did come round he would be a cabbage.

So that was it. He'd gone.

Losing this man who'd been there all through my childhood and my teens, who had given me some stability when I was a kid, was a massive blow. It came at a time when I was struggling with my career and it left me dealing with one of the hardest periods of my life. I felt a bit of a failure, as if I'd let a lot of people down with my performance in the 2010 Tour.

I didn't know how to deal with it. I really struggle to express my emotions and I bury my head in the sand over a lot of stuff. I always try to remain positive even when I'm not feeling it inside. If someone asks me if I'm all right, I'll tend to say, 'Yeah, yeah, I'm fine.' So I tried to take it in my stride, make it look as if I was coping with it. But in fact I was in a bit of a state.

And all that time I'd had no thoughts of

cycling at all; I had been on another planet. My phone had been off since the Tour, so for nearly two and a half weeks people from the team had been trying to ring and they were getting annoyed with me. They were really angry, in fact. They had no idea what had happened. But they were determined that I get back on my bike and get training – and competing – again.

This was my job.

I opted to go to the Grand Prix de Plouay in Brittany, then the British Time Trial Championships and Tour of Britain. But I wasn't really ready.

A week later I went back down to London for George's funeral on the Saturday. I had to race in Brittany the following day but I didn't want to be there. My confidence was already low because I felt as if I had let everyone down during the Tour, so I didn't have the guts at that stage to say, 'I'm not racing, my grandad has just died, it's a hard time for me and I need a week or two off.'

So I got on with it. I finished Plouay, went home and started training again; I was out on my bike every day getting in some decent work. I won the British Time Trial Championships at the start of September, and then I did my job at the **Tour of Britain** but, as a team, we didn't have great form. We won one stage, and I nearly won another, but overall we weren't in the hunt.

For the rest of the season it was a matter of getting through. I felt as if I had no motivation whatsoever.

A massive wake-up call

And then I heard that the Sky team were thinking of replacing me as their team leader.

That really shook me. If Sky replaced me as leader, maybe gave me a team role instead, it would be an admission that I couldn't win the Tour. For in team cycling, the leader is the rider who has the most chance of winning, and much of the work of the other riders is to help get them there – on the podium in first place. So if they dropped me, I would be branded a failure – not up to the task of being at the top of the biggest project that British cycling had ever seen.

The possibility that I might be demoted from leadership, reduced to the ranks, was a massive wake-up call. In a word: humiliation. Dealing with it would mean growing up.

That year I had avoided some of the more stressful responsibilities as team leader – simple things like dealing with the press. I've always had a tendency to withdraw into myself, and that didn't matter when I was an individual on the track going for individual gold medals because I only had to focus on bringing the best out of myself. But Sky is a big outfit. It's not three other guys – like you have in a team pursuit – but twenty-six riders plus thirty-odd staff. If I withdrew as I had often done in the past, it had a bad knock-on effect. So now I needed to make amends. I became a changed man, but I knew I couldn't do it all by myself in terms of training to win the Tour. And there was only one person I knew who could put me on the right footing, who could tell me the things I didn't necessarily want to hear at times when I might not want to hear them.

Only one guy would make me listen.

I went to the team management and I said to them, 'You know what, the only person who really understands me and knows me inside out as a person is you, Shane, and I'd like you to coach me.'

That took Shane aback a little. He said, 'I

wasn't expecting that,' but Dave immediately answered with, 'That's a really good idea, you know.'

That day, I'd been dropped off at the velodrome, planning to do a four-hour ride home. As I got changed at the track, Shane said, 'I'll ride with you for a bit.'

We left the track together and pedalled along for a couple of hours talking.

His initial concerns – he had other commitments too, like running the track programme for British Cycling – were outweighed by his excitement, and his conclusion was that he would coach me on a full-time basis, but with the support of sports scientist Tim Kerrison.

I knew Tim. He had been working at Sky that year – he knew relatively little about cycling, but he had revolutionized training in Australian swimming, and had a lot of good ideas.

I said I would hand the two of them my body: 'Train me,' I said. 'Get the machine working for next July.'

I had unfinished business with the Tour de France.

TIME FOR TRUTH

'This is what I want to do in 2011: I want to start enjoying my racing again – and I want to get back to finishing top ten in the Tour.'

It was the end of November 2010 and my first get-together with the guys who ran the team. I had really thought hard about what I wanted to do at the first training camp for the new season, and here was where it began. I ran through the whole thing, outlining my plan and how I was going to put it into action.

I wasn't going to take no for an answer.

But showing I was serious about 2011 meant

doing more than just talk. I had brought a mountain bike with me to use on the road, all set up with lights and mudguards, and I was out early every morning on it in the freezing cold. Nothing was going to stop me doing my winter training.

I came away from that first training camp feeling good, but it wasn't just down to me. I'd had a meeting with Shane and Tim Kerrison, who had agreed to start helping us.

I really didn't feel very confident in my abilities right now. Could I really make it? Could I ever get back to the heights of 2009? So Tim, Shane and I sat down and deliberately didn't set the bar too high. We were not going to win the Tour de France this year – but we wanted a place in the top ten. It would be a fantastic achievement, and Tim helped me to realize that, physically, I was more than capable of it.

Two minutes – or forty seconds?
They wrote me a winter training programme. And we had a complete change of approach. Tim looked at all the statistics from the 2010 Tour de France. I had had a 'disastrous' race, yet

had still finished 24th – and a lot of people would give their right arm for 24th! He worked out that if I had lost a minute or so less on a lot of my worst days, I would have been up to eleventh. So we started thinking about how I could avoid losing time, and what we realized was that I would be better off riding my own race rather than trying to go with my teammates when they attacked on a climb. My riding style is not explosive – what my body is good at is riding at high intensity for a long time, without ever going completely into the red.

That meant I should drop off the back of the lead group if necessary, when the **climbers** began pushing up the intensity on the mountains. If I rode at my own **tempo** – rode my own race – I would lose maybe only forty seconds. If I tried to stay with the specialist climbers, I could lose as much as two minutes, as I did on one mountain stage in the 2010 Tour.

Two minutes. Or forty seconds. It was a no-brainer.

Top ten in the Tour now felt like an achievable goal.

I believed this could work mainly because I was certain that Shane Sutton was the one person who was not just going to tell me what I wanted to hear. If Shane felt this was a good idea, he really meant it.

It can be infuriating being trained by Shane, because everything in his life is so hectic, but he's constantly thinking of his athletes. He often even puts us before his wife and family!

He is incredibly observant, always watching and thinking. He looks at little details – like the way I am pedalling – and he'll say to me, 'You didn't look comfortable on that climb,' or 'You were pushing too big a gear.'

He is great at knowing when to make an athlete stop and rest too, and one of his favourite sayings is: 'You need to recruit now.' He means that you need to do all the training but you also need to take time off to let your body recover and adapt.

As a coach he is incredibly good at the human side of it. He knows how it feels because he's been there; he knows what six hours in the saddle feels like!

My training programme under Tim and Shane
Since the end of 2010, Tim and Shane have

worked together to plan my training. First, Tim writes the programmes, then Shane adapts them to fit me, based on his experience of bike racing and his knowledge of me. It may seem like they are only small changes, but this attention makes a massive difference to the state of mind of his riders.

For instance, Tim might have pencilled in some interval training three days after I've won a big race; Shane will look at it and say, 'No, Brad just needs to ride his bike that day. He doesn't need the mental stress of doing intervals.'

Between them, Tim and Shane also figure out the areas I need to work on. They look at everything through the year, review what went right and what didn't.

Once we've set the goals and planned what we're doing next year, they go away and write a plan for the season, working back from the main goal – then Tim looks at it for weeks before coming back with a final plan that includes all the details.

For example, a training programme leading up to a main goal of the Tour de France (in July) might mean:

- *Phase one: mid-November to end-December*
  Five weeks' general conditioning, building up to about twenty hours a week

- *Phase two: 1 January to 19 February*
  Pre-race conditioning in Majorca, working harder, starting to touch on threshold areas

- *Phase three: 20 February to 24 March*
  An initial race phase that includes Paris–Nice – a professional cycling stage race held each March and known as the 'race to the sun'

It will be like that all the way towards July. One phase can be two weeks or ten days, another could be a week's rest to 'recruit'.

Shane is hard, but he's honest too. It's always a matter of: 'Right, I'm going to tell you something now – you're not going to like it, and you know I love you to bits, but *these next three days are vital.*' It's like that – he'll tell you you're the best athlete in the world, but you've just got to get this bit right. He'll praise you, but also make sure you understand how important the next stage is. And when you get it wrong, he'll also say: 'I'm telling you, as a mate, that *you messed up big time*, you shouldn't have gone and done what you did, but it's done now and you learn from your mistakes.' But when he tells you that stuff, you know he cares about you. It's why athletes like Sir Chris Hoy and myself are always happy to accept a telling-off from him. He's not ranting at you just because he's had a bad day!

At other times he's surprised me. I've been a bit low physically, needing to recover, but I've still gone out and completed what's on the programme. In that case Shane will say: 'Brad, this is where you've got to be careful, because that's your desire to win the Tour coming through and it may be your downfall; you've still got to be very sensible and listen to your body. Just because you think, "You know what, I'm tired, I'm not going to do it today," that doesn't make you not committed or dedicated to what you're doing.'

Shane has such a reputation as a hard nut that it's quite funny when it's him telling me to take it easier. Usually it's my wife Cath who ends up saying that. I'll say I feel guilty because I didn't go on my bike today and she'll tell me not to be so stupid.

As an athlete you are always trying to find that balance – to walk that fine line between training hard enough and not overdoing it. Getting it right comes partly down to experience – and partly to having the right people around you.

BACK ON TRACK

One of the key things that Shane came up with in autumn 2010 was that I really needed to get back into the velodrome. He feels that track work in the winter gives you real routine, and some of the intense work we do with the Great Britain track squad really helps for the road. So with a view to possibly even riding the team pursuit in the London Olympics – which were now just over eighteen months away – I went back to the GB squad again.

So that was my winter: I would be in the velodrome a couple of times a week doing some fairly intense workouts, then would be riding hard from my home in Lancashire, and that was it.

I did what I had to do, and when I began racing on the road again at the Tour of Qatar, the form was there straight away. That didn't mean I was winning, but it put me in the front group on most of the stages. The team were pleased.

After Qatar it was the track World Cup at Manchester, where I joined up with my fellow Beijing gold medallists Geraint Thomas (or 'G') and Ed Clancy, plus young Steven Burke, for a convincing win that wasn't light years away from the world record we'd set in Beijing. I was getting a lot of praise that winter, which was rewarding after I had made more of an effort to be a leader. Everyone was telling me I was more communicative, a joy to work with again. As an athlete, you feed off that: if you do something and it works and you get positive feedback, you want more of it.

The 2011 season begins . . .
That spring, it all started to go right.

At Paris–Nice – the 'race for the sun' as it is known as the race heads south through France to finish on the sunny Mediterranean coast – I finished third overall. It wasn't run in my kind of weather, being cold and wet (despite the race's name!), and the guys ahead of me – Tony Martin and Andreas Klöden – were both serious stage-race specialists. But it was clearly a step forward – we were heading in the right direction.

And that's how it continued.

At Paris–Roubaix, my favourite one-day Classic of them all, I did a good job for the team, giving Geraint Thomas my wheel when I crashed and he punctured.

At the Tour of Romandie I helped with leading out another of my teammates from the pursuit squad to win a couple of **bunch sprints**.

By that summer, I felt I was beginning to lead the team. I wasn't afraid to make it clear at the start of some events that I was just there for preparation, but I was also ready to give something back by helping my teammates in those races.

Another big change in our approach was that I had begun racing to get results all year round, rather than just putting everything into the Tour. There *are* races out there other than the big one in July. So I thought, holding back for the Tour is not going to change a lot. You've still got to ride the races.

The goal for me, however, was always July; I wanted to peak for my best form in that month, and then go straight on to the London Olympics less than two weeks later, but I wasn't going to sacrifice everything for it. You don't hold any consistent form if you drop off training several times in the year in order to hit one peak after another. It has to be one long build, in which you race as hard as you can, race to win with whatever you've got at the time. If it's good enough for a result, that's great.

The Dauphiné Libéré – riding my own race
I had been 100 per cent committed to the team throughout the season – and then I got the payback at the Dauphiné Libéré, when I put my hand up and said, 'This is a big race for me.'

The Dauphiné is a major event in the second tier of stage races, one rung down from the three big Tours – the Tour de France, the **Giro d'Italia** (in Italy) and the **Vuelta a España** (Spain).

A French cyclist called Jacques Anquetil was the first cyclist to win all three Grand Tours.

DID YOU KNOW?

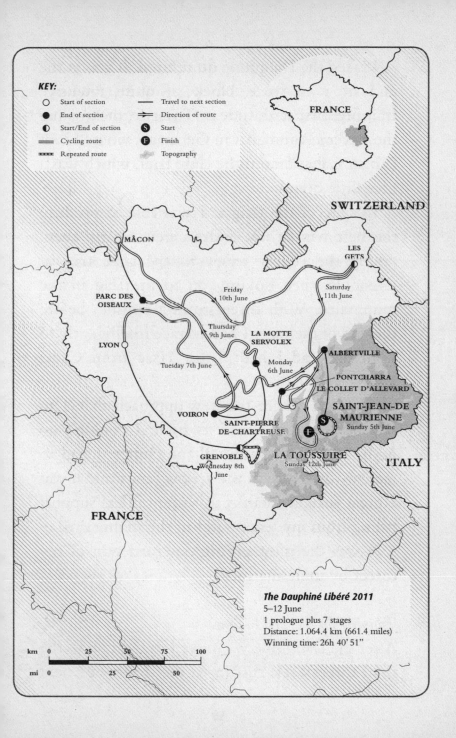

KEY:

○ Start of section
● End of section
◑ Start/End of section
═ Cycling route
⠿ Repeated route
— Travel to next section
⇒ Direction of route
Ⓢ Start
Ⓕ Finish
▨ Topography

FRANCE

SWITZERLAND

MÂCON

LES GETS

PARC DES OISEAUX

Friday 10th June

Saturday 11th June

Thursday 9th June

LA MOTTE SERVOLEX

LYON

Tuesday 7th June

Monday 6th June

ALBERTVILLE

PONTCHARRA

LE COLLET D'ALLEVARD

VOIRON

SAINT-PIERRE DE-CHARTREUSE

SAINT-JEAN-DE MAURIENNE
Sunday 5th June

Ⓢ

Ⓕ

GRENOBLE
Wednesday 8th June

LA TOUSSUIRE
Sunday 12th June

ITALY

FRANCE

km 0   25   50   75   100

mi 0   25   50

The Dauphiné Libéré 2011
5–12 June
1 prologue plus 7 stages
Distance: 1.064.4 km (661.4 miles)
Winning time: 26h 40' 51"

I raced the Dauphiné quite tired. It was at the end of a six-week block of quite intensive training, first at altitude in Tenerife, then racing the Bayern Rundfahrt in Germany, where I beat Fabian Cancellara in the time trial, which was a nice little bonus.

In spite of the fatigue I was able to produce the best win of my entire career up till then, taking the yellow jersey in the time trial at Grenoble, then holding on to the lead in the mountains. With three summit finishes before the end of the race, I had to race intelligently to keep the lead I had: 1min 11sec from Cadel Evans.

This was where the new approach that Tim had devised came into its own: I couldn't go with all the attacks on all the climbs. I had to race my own race in the yellow jersey and it was a great success, thanks to some selfless support riding from my teammates in the mountains.

It was the most prestigious road win of my career by some margin!

Training for the 2011 Tour
After the Dauphiné we moved straight on to the final three-week run in to the Tour: our next

destination was a training camp at altitude in Sestriere in the Italian Alps.

Finishing in the top ten of the Tour looked more than achievable – even getting on the podium seemed to be within reach, but still with the idea of riding my own race.

We had realized that the key thing was to avoid getting involved in the massive explosions at the foot of the climbs when the pure climbers would begin attacking. I had to treat every *col* as if it were a time trial, thinking of getting from A to B as fast as possible without blowing up. It was not the most attractive way to ride a race – not riding with panache – but that was the reality of it.

That was the biggest lesson I learned from the Dauphiné: there was no shame in dropping off the back even if you were wearing the yellow jersey – worn by the race leader – bearing in mind you could always come back to the leaders. Even when I was in yellow, the centre of attention with the cameras watching me, it didn't faze me when I decided the pace was getting too much and I had to put our plan into action, and watching it succeed boosted my confidence as well.

Questions, questions, questions . . .

This change in approach was largely due to the input we had from Tim Kerrison. I'd first met him at the Tour of Britain in 2009 when I had yet to sign for Team Sky but was being kept in the loop about what they were up to. There was a stage that started in Peebles on the Scottish Borders, and Shane turned up with this lad in a Great Britain Swimming fleece – he and Dave had just poached him from the swimming team. Apparently Tim had been on his way to a job interview with English Cricket, but Shane and Dave convinced him to come and work with them. They told him: 'We want to win the Tour, that is our goal, this is what we would like you to do.' And they got him on board before he could go anywhere else.

On paper, Tim's job description was 'performance analyst', but first he had to learn all about bike racing.

In 2010, he spent the year on the road, mainly just observing. He spent all his time in a camper van he and my trainer, Matt Parker, used; I used to call it *the Skip*. Their nickname for it was *Black Betty*, but it was always in a bit of a state!

Tim's not a big talker, but back then you

would never hear him say anything. He was there all the time observing, taking it all in, learning how cycling worked. A key part of that was getting on top of how to interpret the data from **SRMs** – the cranks that measure a cyclist's power output. They are the best way to measure how hard a cyclist is working, and to control the workload in training. Tim wrote a lot of things down. I reckon he could have written a book by the end of that year.

By the end of 2010, though, he had started asking all sorts of questions – simple things that would prove to be more and more important as we went along. It was stuff that an outsider to cycling might ask, such as: 'Why don't the riders warm down at the end of the stage?' He was told there was no scientific reason for not having a warm-down; it was just that no one did it.

He asked more basic questions:

Why is it only the team leader who gets to go on the training camps where we reconnoitre the mountain stages?

Why does only the leader get set blocks of time for training while the rest of the team race themselves to death?

Why don't we get the eight other guys who will race in the Tour – or as many of them as we can – to ride together all year and race in the same races, go to the training camps, check out the mountains together and get to know each other as a football team would?

That single point made me realize that during that first year at Sky we had all raced all over the place. The first time I raced with Geraint Thomas and Edvald Boasson Hagen and all those guys was when we got to the Tour. I'd hardly seen them all year.

Tim was looking at a host of little things that no one had ever questioned before. He was responsible for us beginning to use altitude training camps and he questioned the timings and frequencies of training camps.

Traditionally in professional cycling teams, everyone gets their training bike in January; Tim wanted to know why they couldn't get it in October and then have a training bike that they use at home? And what about specific time-trial bikes?

He went away, looked at the data he had gathered from me and the other riders and worked out what rate you need to be climbing

ALTITUDE TRAINING

Training or living at high altitudes is a tactic many cyclists use to prepare for the mountain-ridden Tour de France. The ability to absorb and process oxygen efficiently is a deciding factor in a racer's performance because it helps them to reach faster speeds for longer. Altitude training helps the rider improve the amount of oxygen delivered to the muscles as the body adapts to the thinner air at mountain tops.

at in the Tour de France. That calculation was done in terms of **VAM** – *velocità ascensionale media* – which translates into English as 'average climbing speed', or how quickly you gain height in a climb. It's basically a measure of how fast you are going upwards, as if you were in a lift, measured in metres per hour.

Tim figured out what power output you needed to be averaging for a certain body weight if you were going to win the Tour. He wrote down all the demands of the event and got me in the lab. We started testing and slowly started to build a picture of what I was capable of doing and what I couldn't do.

The season — and the build-up — continues

As the season went on, as the training and racing and going to altitude took effect, we started to come away with better and better results. The progression was clear:

Third place at Paris–Nice.

A time-trial stage win at Bayern Rundfahrt.

The overall title at the Dauphiné.

We had set off into 2011 with the idea of aiming for a top ten place in the Tour, but eventually we realized that I could be up there with the likes of Cadel Evans and Alexander Vinokourov, who were going for the podium.

There was another aspect that made us more optimistic as the Tour drew closer in 2011. Various things were coming out on the anti-doping front. The UCI – the *Union Cycliste Internationale*, or International Cycling Union – brought in a needle ban, forbidding the use of any injections at all, even for substances used for recovery such as sugars and vitamins.

British Cycling have always had a no-needle policy, but in France you can buy them over the counter; it's a different culture. This kind of development contributes towards a team like ours, which is determined to race clean, coming away with something big at the Tour de France, and Shane kept saying to me that this was all working in our favour. As long as they kept going in that direction, deterring the drug-users – and like all clean athletes, I hate those who use drugs to improve their performances, those that cheat – that would be great.

Cycling weight

As the Tour drew near, I had also dropped to my lightest climbing weight ever: 69 kilos. I'd taken it gradually down to 71.5 by the start of the 2009 Tour. That was 6.5 kilos lighter than I'd been when I rode in 2007. It's important still to eat a healthy, balanced diet, with any athlete working closely with a dietician if they want to tailor a diet to their performance. It takes a good deal of hard work to get it down there, and but it's the most effective way of improving your performance on the road.

DID YOU KNOW?

One kilogram less body weight means you gain about 25 seconds for a given power output on a 30 minute climb.

It's not just about the climbs; every time you accelerate out of a corner or up a little hill you are hefting that extra weight. Over a three-week race those efforts add up to a huge amount of extra work.

On the track you also build up a lot of upper-body muscle, simply due to the work on your arms and shoulders from the standing starts you do. On the road it's not useful and it took a good while to work it off after I switched from track to road racing.

DID YOU KNOW?

To get to the top, Brad eats well. Breakfast is usually a bowl of muesli or porridge, which releases energy slowly. Lunch is often a simple tuna salad sandwich on wholemeal bread. For a snack, a banana or oat and honey energy bars are the favourite choices. Meat and vegetables or pasta are on the menu for dinner, with yoghurt or a small bowl of cereal for an evening snack.

On the podium in Britain
I took first place in the British National Road Race Championships on a super-tough course in the north-east.

I was massively optimistic for the Tour when I faced the press a couple of days before the event. And I raced well to win that national title.

But after that trip to the north-east I got ill – diarrhoea for two days – and as a result, I couldn't travel to the Tour until right up to the last minute. I felt dreadful and was quite close to getting dropped.

The Tour de France 2011

I felt a bit weak when the Tour started, although I got through the first stage in decent shape. I was strong in the team time trial the day after and then I was poised in sixth overall, in a good position for the rest of the week. I always wonder what would have happened once we hit those mountains: whether I would have been in the front or not . . .

On the stage to Châteauroux seven days in, I wasn't well placed in the peloton as we began the final 50km into the finish. As always, everyone was trying to stay in the front. But I kept slipping to the back. I had no fight in me that day.

On the flat stages, you rely on your teammates

THE PELETON

Leading riders of a Grand Tour usually form a tight pack or peloton (French for platoon). Riders save energy by riding close behind others, which reduces wind resistance by up to 40%.

to pull you forward; if the peloton is travelling at 50kph, you have to ride at 55–60kph to overtake the other riders; having someone in front of you to cut through the air means you save energy. With the help of the other guys in Sky, I'd get to the first few rows of the peloton, but then we'd drift back a bit, and I would think, 'I can't be bothered to go round the outside again and fight my way up to the front one more time.' And before you knew it we'd be down the back again.

We're moving up, moving up, moving up, we're about halfway up the field – and then before I know it I'm on the deck! I'm clutching my shoulder, and can't get off the floor without it being agony.

My collarbone is broken.

It's game over.

HOW THE PELOTON WORKS

WIND DIRECTION

Riders bunch up together. Sprinters stay at the back, where there is the least air resistance. This helps them to conserve energy.

But what I'm feeling is weird: the minute I hit the tarmac, I almost feel relieved. Phew, I'm not going to have to see just how good or bad I am . . .

BREAKTHROUGH

When we bought our new house at the end of 2010, one of the things I did early on was get myself a shed in the garden. It's about five metres by five, made of wood, and it's big enough to take a bike and a turbo trainer plus a couple of heaters and a sound system. I can still see the sweat stains on the carpet from the hours I spent in there in August 2011, sitting on the bike, spinning the turbo and dripping like a wet sponge.

But there was no alternative if I wanted to perform in the Tour of Spain – the Vuelta – which ran from mid-August into early Sept-ember.

If I didn't ride the Vuelta, I would have no chance at all of getting anywhere near the podium in the 2012 Tour de France.

I'd never ridden it, so I was kind of looking forward to it. I'd crashed out of the Tour, so I'd be on the comeback trail, which meant there would be no pressure either. I could just go there and race.

Preparing for the Vuelta a España

I had about nine days off after the crash, then I started riding my bike again. Tim put a training programme together for me to get me up to the start. I knew I was still in pretty good shape, as I had been going into the Tour; it wasn't just going to disappear overnight. It was the first real injury I'd had as a pro, the first since I broke my wrist in the winter of 2001.

I kept my weight down, looked after myself and went to the Vuelta with no real ambition other than to race as hard as I could and see what happened.

That was where my shed came into its own. I had no time to go back to altitude after the Tour, and in Lancashire I didn't have any mountains to train in, so a lot of the work was done on the turbo trainer, which is a tripod with a weighted roller on it. You slot your back wheel into the tripod, settle the back tyre on to the roller, then ramp up the resistance to the required level, and you pedal away.

The heat was a massive issue in the Vuelta a España so Tim devised training sessions in a heat chamber – otherwise known as my garden shed! We put heaters in there and a humidifier, getting the temperature up to thirty-five or forty degrees, and I would sit on the turbo for anything up to two hours, just riding the bike . . .

Riding the 2011 Vuelta a España
That Vuelta was funny. I needed those three weeks of racing and I went into it with the attitude, 'Yeah, right, I'll be the team leader, I'll take the responsibility that comes with that, and let's have a crack at it. Maybe I'll end up in the top ten – who knows? Let's see what happens.'

We just took it day by day.

But the first day was terrible. In the team time trial in Benidorm we finished third last, partly because Kurt-Asle Arvesen crashed early

KEY:

- ○ Start of section
- ● End of section
- ◑ Start/End of section
- ═ Cycling route
- ▒ Topography
- — Travel to next section
- ⇒ Direction of route
- Ⓢ Start
- Ⓕ Finish

FRANCE

Avilés
Alto de L'Angliru
La Farrapona Lagos
de Somiedo
Peña
Cabarga
Noja
Bilbao
15
4th September
18
8th September
Intermission
5th September
Solares
19
9th Sept
20
10th September
Vitoria
Sarria
13
2nd Sept
Pontevedra
Astorga
3rd September
14
Haro
Faustino V
12
1st September
Ponteareas
Ponferrada
16
6th September
Villa Romana
La Olmeda
17
7th September
11
31st August

SPAIN

Verín
Intermission
30th August
San Lorenzo
de El Escorial
Salamanca
10
29th August
9
28th August
Villacastín
21
11th September
Ⓕ
MADRID
11th September

PORTUGAL

Sierra de Béjar
La Covatilla
8
27th August
Talavera
de la Reina
7
26th August
Almadén
6
25th August
Úbeda
3
22nd August
La Nucia
1
20th August
Petrer
2
21st August
Ⓢ
BENIDORM
20th August
5
24th August
4
23rd August
Sierra Nevada
Baza
Totana
Playas de Orihuela
Córdoba
Valdepeñas
de Jaén

km 0   100   200   300
mi 0   100   200

The Vuelta a España
20 August–11 September
21 stages
Distance: 3,300km (2,051 miles)
Winning time: 84h 59' 31"

on, which disrupted us all, but basically because we didn't go fast enough.

The next day, Chris Sutton won the stage for us — much better!

Four days in we went up the Sierra Nevada, 2,000m high and the first summit finish I'd done since the Dauphiné; I finished with a front group up there, so that gave us a bit of confidence.

Another five days in — the day before the individual time trial — we had another summit finish, and that was where Chris Froome and I ripped it up. There were just a handful of us left at the top, so we knew we were in the mix, and it went from there.

The day after that we had the time trial at Salamanca. And there, maybe, I made a bit of a mistake: I definitely didn't ride it right, given we were racing at altitude in blistering heat. I finished third behind Tony Martin of Germany and Froomie.

That put Chris in the race lead, but at the next summit finish two days later — a gruelling 19km climb — he slipped back after responding to a series of attacks, and I went with the leaders.

That put me in the leader's jersey, a position

I had never expected to be in. Suddenly I was leading the race and looking as if I was one of the best guys there. And I started to think: *I can win this.*

But in the last week there's a finish that's one of the hardest and steepest in bike racing. For nearly four miles the climbs are averaging a gradient of one-in-seven; there's one section where it is close to one-in-four, and other bits are around one-in-five! That's steep!

I still finished fifth there, but that's where my weakness showed – it was just too severe for where I was physically.

From that point on, the race became about keeping a place on the podium, which I managed, running out third overall behind Juan José Cobo of Spain and Froomie.

Merely getting on the podium was a success in itself, although it was a huge disappointment at the time to me as I'd started to believe I could win. However, looking back at where I'd come from, third wasn't too bad. And it was from that point on I thought: 'Well, if I get the preparation right next year, and I don't have a broken collarbone for six weeks before it, maybe I can win the Tour . . .'

Top Left: Me and my dad, Gary. He was a decent cyclist in his day

Top Right: Getting to grips with an early time-trial bike

Above: Me as a young lad

Left: Even as a young boy, I always loved cycling

FACING PAGE:

Top: One of my first ever races!

Bottom left: Other kids were into football, but my bedroom walls were filled with posters of my cycling heroes, like Indurain and Museeuw

Bottom right: Too cool for school

THIS PAGE:

Right: Triumphant after the individual pursuit in the Beijing 2008 Olympics

Left: Lap of honour in the Sydney 2000 Olympics with Paul Manning, Chris Newton and Bryan Steel

Bottom left: Fighting back with Rob Hayles in the Madison in Athens after Rob's crash

Bottom right: The 2010 Tour de France was a struggle, although Cadel Evans (left) doesn't seem to be finding it easy either!

PREVIOUS PAGE: Where's Wiggo! See if you can spot me at the start of the 2011 Tour . . .

THIS PAGE:

Left: Cav triumphs in Copenhagen, one of the proudest days of my cycling career

Below: I'm leading the train with Steve Cummings and G on my wheel

FACING PAGE: Waiting at the start in the peloton

Above: Being greeted by a great crowd

Right: 'I didn't want to look back in ten years' time and wonder what I might have achieved. I don't want to have any regrets.'

Training lessons learned

After the Vuelta I felt like a completely different rider. I'd got my first podium finish in a Grand Tour – a very big step in a mountainous race, especially after breaking a collarbone and being restricted in what training I could manage beforehand.

I'd proved that I was capable of racing as well as I had in 2009. That had been a big question mark up to that point: *was I ever going to get back to that level?* What's more, I'd done it in a different race, and one that was extremely tough.

We had also made a massive discovery. The conventional wisdom in cycling is that you need a decent number of days of racing in your legs before you go into a three-week stage race, but because of my collarbone we had had no option other than to go against that. After the Dauphiné in early June I had raced just seven days before I started the Vuelta: one day at the British National Championships and six at the Tour. On paper it didn't look good for Spain, but what we found out that August and September was that as long as the training is right, you perhaps don't have to race as much as you might expect.

Shane and Tim had introduced me to TrainingPeaks, which is an online coaching platform that enables the coaches to communicate with the riders. From the start of 2011, all my data went on to it – I would download all the information on every training session from my SRM cranks – which measure power output – while the SRM unit also measures pulse rate, pedalling **cadence**, speed etc. The software gives you what they call **TSS** – *Training Stress Scores* – showing how hard you've been working.

Here's an even more important point we realized: the fitter you get, the less the races take it out of you – which in turn would mean you'd have to train even harder.

The Vuelta was the eye-opener: I'd finished third after three and a half weeks of quality training. And the training hadn't even been about the Vuelta – we only went there to prepare for the World Time Trial Championships.

So now the plan was: don't go to the race to train, but train first, go to fewer races – and *go there to win*.

BROTHERS IN ARMS

Closing the season

Coming up next were two big jobs to be done in Copenhagen.

First up, the World Time Trial Championships – a race I'd never quite got right.

For a good five years, Fabian Cancellara had been the man to beat in time trials, the best in the world by some margin. He'd won the World Championships in 2006, 2007, 2009 and 2010 (he didn't ride in 2008), and Olympic gold in 2008. It was only in 2011 that people started to get the better of him.

At the World's in 2011 in Copenhagen, Tony Martin of Germany took gold and I rode to silver – it was the first time Cancellara had been beaten in the championships since 2005. That made the time trial a huge day for me and closed the season brilliantly.

But there was another job still to do on the Sunday – a team job to help Cav win the sprint.

Cav – king of the sprinters

The first time I remember bumping into Mark Cavendish was in the corridor at the Manchester velodrome some time in 2003 when I was in there training for the World Pursuit Championship. Cav was in the academy – he'd have been seventeen or maybe eighteen.

By 2007 he had turned pro, got his first big win and he was getting established as a sprinter. We both rode the 2007 Tour, then started doing some six-days together that winter as preparation for the Madison at the World's and the Olympics, and spent a lot of time at training camps and races.

Cav is like my younger brother. We fall out, we make up, we take the mickey out of each other, say this and that – but the relationship is never going to go away now.

MARK CAVENDISH

Cavendish is known for his sprinting and has been named the Tour de France's best sprinter of all time by French newspaper *L'Equipe*. He is fourth on the all-time Tour de France winners list, having won 23 stages.

NATIONALITY British

BORN 1985

HEIGHT 1.75m (5ft 9in)

WEIGHT 69kg (150lb)

RIDER TYPE Sprinter

In 2008 we won the Madison together at the World Championships, and then it was the Beijing Olympics, where the Madison was a disaster because I wasn't at my best, and Cav was extremely unhappy as it was his only chance for a medal and he was really pumped for it.

After Beijing, I didn't speak to him until I saw him in Qatar the following February, but we never mention the Olympics when we talk – it's just something we have never, ever discussed.

In years to come, I know I'll look back and be proud to tell my grandchildren I rode with Mark Cavendish, the greatest sprinter of all time. A large part of that comes from the World Road Race Championships in Copenhagen, where the Great Britain lads put in one of the most dominating rides that event has ever seen . . .

The World Road Race Championships,
September 2011
I got my medal in the time trial, and then in the road race I had a role to play. My job was to do the last lap, to keep the pace as high as I could, and make sure that the peloton was all together

when the final build-up to the sprint began.

During the race, there wasn't a lot of time to take it in. We had jobs to do, so we were concentrating on remembering the plan. Personally, I was just counting down the kilometres until I could open up. I felt the urge to go early. I was constantly thinking, 'I'm going to go now.'

David Millar was the one who was captaining the team on the road that day; he was always sitting behind me and he was continually talking to me: 'Not yet, Brad, it's too early, we need you on the last lap, wait, wait, wait, wait . . .' Dave was instrumental in our success; his guiding role was superb. He kept me on a leash. I didn't want to be in a fight on the last lap – without him I'd have gone too early and ripped the race to bits.

On the last lap I was able to go for it. That turn I did felt fantastic. I was just super light on the bike. I always thought I had it in me but I had that rare feeling of grace, of confidence. I was convinced that no one would be coming past me – I had that kind of cocky attitude, and I was swerving across the road going into the climbs, messing up any accelerations from behind. I didn't expect to last as long as I did – I think I did 8 or 10km on the front, and at the end I felt incredibly proud that I'd committed to the job and I'd done it. I hadn't let Cav down.

Then I crossed the line and realized that we'd won and that sparked off a whole different set of feelings.

We were all a bit dumbstruck, all a bit in shock. I don't think we fully appreciated what we'd achieved. Cav's gold medal was a victory for all of us. But this time it was much, much more for me – I did it for Cav. Since mid-2011, with him it has always felt special. He's so gracious, so grateful for everything you do for him. When you are committing to do your job for him, you know he's not going to let you down. That's inspiring in a way because you know he really needs you on the road when you're doing your utmost.

The spirit that we built for that race was special, and it had come through when we had the team meeting before the start. We had to discuss what would happen if Cav punctured in the last lap. We began wondering whether we should try and set up the finish for Geraint

Thomas or something like that but I said, 'Look, we start as a team, we'll finish as a team. We're all here for Cav, we've all agreed to ride the World's to help Cav win. If we do the whole day for Cav and he punctures on the last lap, we all stop, we all wait and we all try to get back. We'll finish as a team that way.'

The attitude in that team was the same as if we had been going into war. We weren't going to leave anyone out there on the battlefield!

That week in Copenhagen was just the best way to end the season. Afterwards, Shane was emphatic: 'Just five weeks off now – don't touch your bike for five weeks. When we come back in November we're starting properly.'

I had to be ready to start training hard on 1 November 2011. That was when the 2012 season *really* began.

Two jerseys?
Moves had been afoot to bring Cav to Sky for a while and eventually he did sign, and all at once the game changed: the questions started about whether we were going to try and win both the yellow and the green jerseys in the

Tour de France – a massive task for any team to take on.

It started becoming obvious in January that we were going to try to win both – so the questions started again: 'Is it possible? Can you do it? Can you win yellow and green in the same Tour?'

TEARING UP TRADITION

There's a stiff breeze blowing in central France as we head towards Orléans on the second stage of Paris–Nice, but I'm already on cloud nine. I'm lying second overall after the prologue time trial. This stage is about sustained vigilance. I have to keep my eyes open and not get caught.

Sure enough, the gaps begin to open at the front. We've got about 100km to race, we're on a typical French route nationale, dead straight with trees perfectly spaced every 20m and a farm building every couple of kilometres. Vacansoleil are the team who commit first, driving at the front.

Almost the whole peloton goes into the left-hand gutter to try and keep out of the wind. As most of the guys immediately dive left, those who've got the strength try and go into the wind down the right to get into the first group. There are about twenty or twenty-five pulling clear, the next echelon not closing on them.

If I want to win Paris–Nice, I need to be in that front group.

I'm about forty riders back; I'd rather go up the outside even if I'm fighting against the wind: it's better than trying to hide in a wheel. So I go right to find the open road.

I'm sprinting up to the back of the front group, across the gap to the back of the line; keep looking at those wheels a few metres in front of me, and that's it, I'm there. I'm where I need to be.

On a windy day, once you're in the front group it's simple – it's making it there that's the hardest bit.

The last intermediate sprint comes up, and I get myself in the right place to start sprinting for it; I don't quite know why. Whether I get that sprint or not, I can take the jersey at the end of the stage, and there is still the time trial on the last day.

The sprint comes into view; no one else is going for it, so I give it a push, and that's a useful two-second time bonus in the bag . . .

My form is better than it has ever been. But we're working towards July. I haven't peaked for Paris–Nice. This is all part of the process.

Winter training

The 'Race to the Sun' was where the winning streak of 2012 began, but the process of getting there started five months earlier, on 1 November 2011. After the World Championships in Copenhagen, I took five weeks off, and then, on 1 November, I was ready to train again.

- First week: fifteen hours' riding
- Second week: eighteen hours
- Third week, twenty-one

Before I knew it, we'd got to Christmas and I'd put in nine weeks of good, consistent, on-the-ball training.

Sky went to Majorca the week before Christmas for the team training camp and I turned the wick up a bit: forty hours in seven days out there – six hours a day with Eddie

Boasson Hagen. For someone who works in an office, that's like pedalling every hour of the working day!

I didn't just spend that winter on the bike though. I was also in the gym three days a week from six a.m., working to a strength programme devised for me by Mark Simpson, British Cycling's conditioning coach at the time.

After having broken my collarbone, my left arm was very weak, and that meant I couldn't work hard enough when climbing out of the saddle. All-round, I didn't have enough upper-body strength to deal with the steepest climbs.

It's always been known that steep climbs aren't for me; I struggle on them. But Tim and Shane's view was that at some point I was going to have to perform on those climbs if I wanted to win the biggest race. My answer was that I've never been great at it – I had always been known for my good pedalling speed on the track.

To perform on some of these steep climbs, you have to work on your power and your **torque** – producing that power at a lower cadence. That was why we started doing torque sessions for time trialling, and I had to get to the gym. It was not only to get the power back in my left arm, but also just to increase my general physical fitness and strength. I had to do it without bulking up – becoming stronger physically but not putting any muscle on.

I felt a huge difference straight away and the gym work was a classic case of the three of us working out where I had a weakness and refusing to accept it. A lot of athletes will simply accept that they aren't so good in certain areas rather than trying to do anything about it. But the art is to work on your weak areas without losing what you're good at – and that's very much what we achieved in 2012. I used to really struggle when the climbers started attacking at the foot of a mountain – I lacked the explosive power to deal with it – so why not deal with it?

This change in attitude came partly from Tim asking all his questions as a non-cyclist coming in from another sport. Cycling is very traditional and set in its ways about how you train. Since I was a kid it had always been the same:

- October/November – time off
- 1 December – start training
- January – up the miles
- February/March – enter your first races

That is the tradition of cycling. But Tim had come along and asked why we didn't train at the same high level for twelve months of the year – like swimmers or rowers.

The attitude I took to my training had changed a lot too. I said to Shane and Tim at the end of 2011, 'I don't care what you ask me to do, I have a lot of faith in you because we've come on a lot this year. I just want to win the Tour de France.' I didn't know how long I would be able to go on training for the Tour and living the life it demands – it's very intense and takes a huge toll on your life and on everyone else around you – but I felt I was willing to give it a shot in 2012, because I had a decent chance to win the Tour and I might never win it again.

This might be my one opportunity.

Using TrainingPeaks, Tim began to work out my training for the day – times, power outputs, cadences – he would upload it, and tell me to go and read it in an email. It's a far cry from the mileage chart that they used to print on the *Cycling Weekly* centre-spread at Christmas every year, which I coloured in religiously until I was about sixteen!

So the schedules came in, week by week. I did exactly what I was asked, then each day I downloaded the file from the box on the handlebars – the little computer that records all the data – and put it into TrainingPeaks for Tim to look at.

I wasn't interested in the details. I had 100 per cent faith in what Tim and Shane put down on paper. I gave them total responsibility.

Which races?
In the midst of all that we also came up with a race programme, and together we decided that I should race less in 2012.

In Pro Cycling, the World Tour brings together the biggest road races – from the three-weekers to **One-Day Classics**. We worked back from the Tour and planned the programme.

Then we thought: 'What are my goals in those races?' And the plan we came up with – my goals for the year – was:

CYCLING CALENDAR:
UCI World Tour

JANUARY

Tour Down Under (Stage) Australia

FEBRUARY

MARCH

Paris–Nice (Stage) France
Tirreno–Adriatico (Stage) Italy
Volta a Catalunya (Stage) Spain
Milan–San Remo
(Monument One Day) Italy
E3 Harelbeke (One Day) Belgium
Gent–Wevelgem (One Day) Belgium

APRIL

Vuelta al Pais Vasco (Stage) Spain
Tour de Romandie (Stage) Switzerland
Tour of Flanders
(Monument One Day) Belgium
Paris–Roubaix
(Monument One Day) France
Liège–Bastogne–Liège
(Monument One Day) Belgium
Amstel Gold Race (One Day)
The Netherlands
La Flèche Wallonne (One Day) Belgium

MAY

Giro d'Italia (Grand Tour) Italy

JUNE

The Dauphiné Libéré (Stage) France
Tour de Suisse (Stage) Switzerland

JULY

Tour de France (Grand Tour)

AUGUST

Tour de Pologne (Stage) Poland
Eneco Tour (Stage) The Netherlands
Clásica de San Sebastián (One Day) Spain
Vattenfall Cyclassics (One Day) Germany
GP Ouest-France (One Day) France

SEPTEMBER

Vuelta a España (Grand Tour) Spain

Giro di Lombardia
(Monument One Day) Italy

Grand Prix Cycliste de Québec
(One Day) Canada

Grand Prix Cycliste de Montréal
(One Day) Canada

OCTOBER

Tour of Beijing (Stage) China

NOVEMBER

DECEMBER

Tour of Algarve: to play a team role but try and win the time trial.

Paris–Nice: I was third last year, so I really wanted to have a crack at that, and go for the overall classification. I said, 'I'll accept responsibility as leader.'

Tour of Catalonia: a team role again.

Romandie: I wanted to win.

Dauphiné: a win.

Paris–Nice, Romandie and Dauphiné are all only five, six or seven days long, so it's not as if you've got to lead for three weeks each time. The idea was to go to those races, perform, treat each one as if it were a Tour de France in miniature, lead the race and get the team around me to do the job as they would in the Tour.

When it came to July, getting it right wasn't just a matter of being in perfect form – it was as much about leading the team and getting used to leading overall and all that went with it.

So, how did I do?

Tour of Algarve

I won the time trial – by less than a second – from Tony Martin; Richie Porte from Sky won the overall, and I was third. It was key to help the other guys like Richie win in their own right – their sacrifice was going to be a huge part of me winning the Tour de France. I had to think of the bigger picture; I was in a team role, and I had to act like it – my teammates had to realize that if I said I would ride in a certain way, that's what I would do.

Paris–Nice

This was more than just a physical test. There were other things that I was worried about more than the climbing and the time trials. The route wasn't the problem; the issue was that I really struggle in cold weather, and on some days it didn't get above zero all day. Simply staying warm enough so that I didn't crack was a bigger challenge than the physical demands of racing. The cold and wet is something I've always struggled with – I've no idea why. Some people prefer it but I find it affects my legs more than anything; once they go cold, or they get wet from the rain, they just shut down.

The race was everything to me at the time. I was racing for those six or seven days with no thought about the Tour. I wanted to win that week, and that was that.

At Paris–Nice I was still two or three kilos over the weight I wanted to be in July – that gave me a little more explosiveness, and the weight I was at that time was good for the weather. Having the extra kilos on meant I wasn't getting as cold and it didn't matter because we didn't have to go up climbs for thirty, forty, fifty minutes on end. The Paris–Nice climbs were more explosive, short 2 or 3km ascents.

As usual in a stage race, once I'd got the lead it was just a matter of going day by day, the team taking the strain, then I was finishing it off at the end; keeping in touch on the bunch finishes, hanging in on the big climb at the end of the stage to Mende.

What wins you the Tour is all the work you put in over the whole year, all the background training. That is what allows you to be at your best for twenty-one days in July without having one bad day. At the form I was in for Paris–Nice in 2012, I might have been good enough to come fourth in the Tour, but obviously it's that last five per cent that's going to push you onto the podium in the Tour. And that last few per cent was going to come from the fine-tuning, working with the dietician to get to my perfect weight for the event, being acclimatized to altitude, being acclimatized to the heat. That's what gives you the ability to race day after day for three weeks the seven, eight months of training before it.

Tour of Catalonia

After Paris–Nice, we had a week off, then we went to Catalonia; there it was just a case of riding the race and letting the mountainous terrain give me a workout.

This should have been a classic example of using a race as training, but it went belly up when the final stages were snowed off.

So I went home and Tim devised three tough six-hour rides for me instead!

Romandie

We went away and did an altitude camp, so by the time I got back to Romandie I was ready to go again.

Romandie is five days' work, then it's all over, and after that we had five weeks to the Dauphiné.

The idea of racing yourself fit is a curious one. What Tim identified is that when you race a lot, there are times when you don't work your body hard enough. You *de-train*. The trouble with racing is that sometimes mentally you can't be bothered to compete to the max so you just sit in the peloton and it becomes a way of getting the hours in, cruising along – it can end up a bit like sitting on the turbo trainers.

That's even the case in the Tour. The first few days of the Tour should be relatively easy, sitting in the peloton for 200km in a flat stage. If there's a wind or bad weather that changes it, but the first 200km you're just sitting in, chatting with your mates. It's only the last 50km that are hard because you have to stay in position as the speed goes up massively. You could go out and do a five-hour training ride harder than that!

Clearly, we got our preparation for the Tour spot on, but what made all the difference was having people like Tim in the background, asking those questions. Building up to the Tour was about defying tradition, not being scared to try out new ideas. That was always Dave Brailsford's goal for the team: changing the way we think, defying received ideas, asking why it's always been done like this.

The most obvious example is warming down at the end of the stage. How many teams are doing that now? But when we started warming down in 2011 everyone laughed: 'What are they doing? Look at them idiots.' But it makes total sense: you warm up, so why not warm down?

I think we're setting a precedent for how it's done in the future.

Up in the mountains
Another radical change! Two-week training camps at altitude in Tenerife in the Canaries, staying on top of Mount Teide, the volcano in the middle of the island. We did one camp in April, but the second one in mid to late May, six weeks before the Tour, was probably the most important. Quite a lot of Tour de France mountain stages finish high up, so the main goal was to be able to perform at altitude without any drop-off in power.

The Tour went over 1,600m eleven times during the three weeks, and Tim said, 'We've got to train for altitude.' But he was also asking the question: 'What do we need to *do* at altitude? If we're going to Tenerife for two weeks we've got to know what we're doing.' So he went to Tenerife in January, went around all the roads, looked into how other people were training at altitude and came up with plans of what he thought we should do. He really did his homework.

From each camp we did at altitude, we seemed to be getting a bit more information to make the next one better. There is a difference between *training* at altitude, which can be pretty damaging, and *acclimatization* to altitude, where you just let your body adapt to the thinner air.

There is a well-known benefit from being at altitude: as your body adapts, it naturally produces more red blood cells, increasing your body's capacity to carry oxygen to the muscles and therefore improving your performance. This is what most people think of as 'altitude training', but this wasn't our goal. What we wanted to do in 2012 was acclimatize – get our bodies used to performing in that thin air so that we would all be able to do it at the Tour.

The goal in the plan was to do 100,000m of climbing between March and June. That sums up that period. If you worked it out it was about 10,000m a week — a little bit more than the equivalent of going from sea level to the top of Everest!

But it was clear to me that if I was going to win the Tour I was going to have to do a lot of climbing. At first just going up the hills would help in itself, but later on the work I had to do on those climbs was very specific. In Tenerife in April, we were doing five or six hours a day. It's the kind of climbing you'll do on the Tour on the first climb of the day, when a team is riding tempo on the front and there are three cols to go.

At the second camp, in the big, intense sessions, we might do as much as an hour and a half of threshold, working at the point where your body is producing lactate as fast as it can process it — in other words, the point where if you go any harder you crack rapidly. That was all on climbs: pure hard work.

The critical thing is that I couldn't have done any of this without all the background training going back to November. I was able to train hard, but I didn't dig myself into such a hole that I needed a week off when I got back. That is part of the philosophy that swimmers train to: daily grind.

And it's very hard work.

But after one of those rides we do in Tenerife you feel incredible satisfaction. The last stint we did there was twenty-five minutes, starting at 1,500m altitude and going to 2,200.

We planned to ride:

- one minute at 550 **watts** – basically prologue power, which you can sustain for a few minutes. Normal cadence, high power.
- then four minutes at threshold torque – 50rpm at threshold, maybe 400–440 watts depending on the altitude, which is like going up a steep hill in your car with your foot to the floor in fourth. Low cadence, threshold power.

Then we started again . . . So, five sets of five minutes. We'd already done five and a half hours – one hour at threshold – so the last five minutes were horrible; you're at 2,000m and you can hardly breathe, but you know that in the Tour you will be glad you've put yourself through this.

It's hard to put into layman's terms how you feel. It's a nice way of being totally knackered. And when you are fit and your form is great, those efforts are hard in a very sweet way.

Training to win the Tour takes a lot of sacrifice in all our lives – including your family. But you get to a point in your career where you tell yourself you are no longer going to compromise.

I didn't want to look back in ten years' time and wonder what I might have achieved.

I don't want to have any regrets.

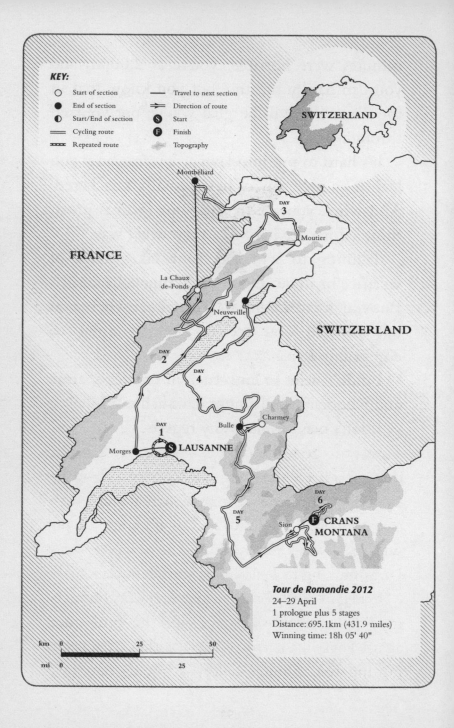

KEY:

○ Start of section
● End of section
◑ Start/End of section
═ Cycling route
▥ Repeated route

— Travel to next section
⇒ Direction of route
Ⓢ Start
Ⓕ Finish
░ Topography

SWITZERLAND

Montbéliard

DAY 3

Moutier

FRANCE

La Chaux de-Fonds

La Neuveville

SWITZERLAND

DAY 2

DAY 4

Charmey

Bulle

DAY 1

Morges Ⓢ LAUSANNE

DAY 6

DAY 5

Sion Ⓕ CRANS MONTANA

Tour de Romandie 2012
24–29 April
1 prologue plus 5 stages
Distance: 695.1km (431.9 miles)
Winning time: 18h 05' 40"

km 0   25   50

mi 0   25

THE MIDAS TOUCH

The Tour of Romandie

I couldn't help feeling that something special might be on its way. I was growing in confidence, and at times, what was happening seemed almost too good to be true. There were days on those roads on the west side of Switzerland in late April when everything I touched seemed to turn to gold. Sometimes I felt as if I could do no wrong. It was a feeling I had never had before. I was starting to feel almost untouchable.

It began well for us when Geraint Thomas used his pursuit skills to win the prologue; again I was a victim of the weather. It started raining ten minutes before I got to the start line, and I finished eleventh. Without that, I'd have been very close to Gee, so from that moment on I knew I was in good shape. But it was on the first stage when eyebrows were raised as I managed something I hadn't achieved since I was an amateur – I won a bunch sprint.

That day was a tough stage. We went up some decent climbs in the finale and it whittled the group down quite a bit. There weren't many bodies left at the end, so I put the boys on the front early on to ride tempo behind the break. When a team does that it's always a statement of intent – 'We're going to take responsibility and try to win this.' It was an example of how I was beginning to ride like a leader too: I put my hand up, saying, 'I want to win it, I will take the responsibility.'

We lost Cav over the climbs, so he wasn't there to go for the sprint finish. The peloton lined up for the stage finish with about 3km to go; I was about fourth wheel behind a little train from the Rabobank team. We got into the final kilometre and no one came past, so I thought, 'That's it; I'm going.' I put my foot down at 500m from the line, just went as hard as I could, and that was that.

It was a good ten years since I'd won a race in that way and the win earned me a useful time bonus that put me in the leader's jersey for day two. I was surprised at the win: I knew I was fast enough to win a sprint, knew I had the length for it – it was about a 20 sec push, and in training we do up to a minute in those efforts – but I was amazed that having led out for so long no one came round me. I was surprised, too, that people didn't realize I had that kind of speed in me from racing on the track. After all, that was the same kind of flat-out effort I would make when we were full on in a Madison event.

It was a new experience. I'd never won a road stage at a major race – I was always thought of as a time-trial specialist, and generally, I can't stand bunch sprints. But when you win in that fashion there's an element of adrenaline – a real rush – because it all happens so quickly. You don't know you're going to win until a few metres before the line, whereas in a time trial you've got a long time to think, 'I'm going to win this, I'm still the fastest time, I'm going to win this . . .' In the sprint, I had much more of the feeling of racing my bike – the race was on for the last 20 or 30km, and I won it. It felt like being a junior again.

Romandie was Sky's best performance as a unit in any stage race since we had started out as a team. We dominated all week: Gee won the prologue, I won two stages, and Richie Porte and Mick Rogers finished third and fifth overall behind me.

The five days were a good test for a rider preparing to go for the overall at the Tour de France – an uphill time trial, a prologue and some hilly stages. I had to nail the final time trial as well to regain the lead from Luis León Sánchez of Rabobank, who had won the penultimate stage to take the jersey from me.

The time trial was 16.5km – but it wasn't flat. On paper I had a good chance of taking back the 10sec I needed to win overall, but nothing could be taken for granted. The climb up towards the finish was a tough one, and my chain came off at the bottom, as I shifted from the big chain ring to the little one to get into a lower gear. I tried to flick the chain back on by hand, but it wouldn't go, so I had to stop and let the mechanic do it. In the past I'd have lost my temper and bunged the bike into the ravine by the road, but this was different. In 2009 at the World Time Trial Championship in Switzerland exactly the same thing happened – my chain went and that time I chucked the bike away in disgust. Here, I remember thinking, 'This could happen in the Tour, deal with it.' So I did. I went on to beat Luis León by 1min 23sec, and it earned me my second major stage race of the season.

You either react to incidents of this kind in the way that I did, or you lose it. That's a mind-set, a pathway. Keeping an eye on the bigger picture shows your focus and confidence. There's also an element of taking responsibility as a leader for everything you do. After the work the team had done, paying them back by throwing my bike on the ground wouldn't have gone down well!

The chain derailing was a small incident at the time but, looking back, it seems like a significant milestone.

There was no big deal made of any of the wins; it all just felt as if it was meant to be. It was like being in a football team in mid-season: great victory, but we're playing Manchester

United or Chelsea next week! But I was pretty tired after Romandie. We'd had a massive April; we'd done a lot of hours, and I had had only five days at home to recover before we travelled there. As a result, I didn't feel great in Switzerland even though it went so well. I wasn't comfortable and had to dig deep at times, for example to win that first road stage. But that was the plan: the early season wasn't about winning Romandie – it was about building to be at my best at the Tour.

I had a massive downer after Romandie. I felt like packing it all in, simply because I looked at Twitter, and while social media is a great way to keep in touch on the net, it has a downside that most people in the public eye experience: users can say pretty much whatever they like about you under the cover of a pseudonym. They can target you, but you don't know who they are.

And it was about this time that a group of people 'out there' began making insinuations about drugs. I started thinking that I didn't want to win the Dauphiné Libéré, because if I did win it they would say that I was doping. Then I began thinking: 'Imagine if I win the

Tour – what will they come up with then?' I spoke to Shane; he got pretty annoyed and said to me – among other things – 'You have just got to ignore those people.' I said, 'Yeah, but I'm human. I can't just take it on the chin all of the time.'

I immersed myself in time with my family and, as usual, it was my wife Cath who took the brunt of my doubts. We began to realize that it was part of dealing with success. There is a lot of other stuff that comes with winning bike races. I look back now and I think: 'Well, maybe that's part of the process, maybe it's not just about leading races but about dealing with all the other hassle that comes with it.'

The Dauphiné Libéré 2012

The Critérium du Dauphiné, or Dauphiné Libéré as cycling traditionalists call it, was not quite like the other events I'd raced in 2012. It was the moment when the season became truly serious. We came to the start in Grenoble after a two-week training camp in Tenerife, and we all knew that now we were into the last period before the Tour.

I was already the Tour favourite, but the other Tour big names for July – Cadel Evans, Vincenzo Nibali and Andy Schleck – were all going to be riding at the Dauphiné. This all put the Dauphiné at a different level compared to the other races. In addition, for the first time in my career on the road I was going back as defending champion to a stage race I had won.

It felt different from the minute we started the prologue. I was last off, because of being the previous year's winner, which was a new experience altogether. There were thunderstorms, and although I had a dry run the wind had changed quite a bit, so in the circumstances finishing second by one second to Luke Durbridge of Australia was a good enough ride, and I'd gone considerably faster than everyone who'd started around me.

The next day was a little different: Cadel won the stage after getting away close to the end, but he wasn't far ahead and I took the race leader's jersey.

I knew that my time-trialling form was there from the prologue – and I was even more certain after day five, the 42.5km *contre-la-montre* to

CADEL EVANS

Winner of the 2011 Tour de France, Cadel Evans was the first Australian winner in Tour history.

NATIONALITY Australian

BORN 1977

HEIGHT 1.74m (5ft 9in)

WEIGHT 67kg (150lb)

RIDER TYPE All-rounder

VINCENZO NIBALI

Known as 'the shark', Nibali's biggest win to date is the overall in the 2012 Vuelta a España.

NATIONALITY Italian

BORN 1984

HEIGHT 1.80m (5ft 11in)

WEIGHT 63kg (140lb)

RIDER TYPE All-rounder

ANDY SCHLECK

Schleck was awarded the 2010 Tour de France yellow jersey after Alberto Contador's disqualification. Schleck also won the Young Rider classification three times at the Tour de France and once at the Giro d'Italia.

NATIONALITY Italian

BORN 1984

HEIGHT 1.80m (5ft 11in)

WEIGHT 63kg (140lb)

RIDER TYPE Climber

Bourg-en-Bresse. I nearly caught Cadel, who had started two minutes ahead of me, and that felt like the first time I had really put the hammer down before the Tour. As far as the time trial itself went, it was ridiculously windy – the worst I've ever done – and at times I was right on the limit of being blown off. You didn't dare even to take your hands off the bars to take a drink of water. Andy Schleck did come unstuck in the wind, breaking his pelvis, which put him out of the Tour.

I hadn't set out to catch Cadel – I always expect to catch the rider in front of me, but that simply reflects the state of mind I have for every time trial I ride, and there were some lovely long straights on the course. I had him in sight for a long time in those final kilometres, but I still kept to my rhythm – I didn't want to take too many risks on corners – and he finished strongly. It's not a case of thinking, 'Oh yes, I'll catch him now'; at that point you are both trying to empty the tank. All you can do is ride your own race.

After that we had only to defend the jersey. The real statement for the Tour came on the second-to-last stage – a full-scale day in the

HOW A TEAM RIDES A CLIMB

WIND DIRECTION

1: The team forms a line, with the climbing specialists at the front. Climbing specialists are skilled in choosing the best line on a climb, and setting the pace for the other riders. Climbing specialists typically have a lightweight physique and specifically developed muscles.

2: They will each take it in turns to lead the team for a short distance. Although the team's average speed will typically drop during a prolonged climb, there is still an aerodynamic advantage to slipstreaming or drafting.

Alps culminating in the Col de Joux Plane; a brute of a climb which is shorter than the usual Alpine col at just over seven miles, but hits a gradient of one-in-nine in places. The bottom of the mountain was almost impossibly hard, with Eddie setting an incredible pace. After that it was a matter of the team riding as they had done in training in Tenerife, where we had practised this: hitting a climb, three guys in front of me, each of them doing 3km as hard and as long as they're capable of, and then peeling off.

Because I was sitting in second or third wheel all the way up the climb, I never turned round. I try never to look behind on a climb, so that all the other riders get to see is my backside. You don't need to assess the others: if you're feeling it then they're feeling it!

As I've often said, I know my cycling history. So the night I won the Dauphiné, I knew I had a new record. No one had ever won Romandie, Paris–Nice and Dauphiné in the same year – that little record of mine made me hugely proud.

But after the Dauphiné one part of the bigger picture became clear: we had an incredible team for the Tour de France and I was going to be the favourite.

Everyone was saying it.

I knew it.

I would have to deal with it.

THE WINGMEN – AND A WORKING-CLASS HERO

The Tour team

There wasn't that much to be decided about the team that Sky chose for the Tour. The core group that had trained and raced with me all year selected itself, and as a star in his own right Cav was always going to be added to that list.

There was, however, some debate among the selection panel about whether or not the ninth rider should be Bernhard Eisel, Cav's right-hand man. The issue confronting the selection panel went back to the question that had been asked when Cav was signed: *could we race for both green and yellow?* As the season went on it became more and more clear that I was the favourite for the Tour. Bringing Cav to the Tour raised the question of who they should bring to back him up, and in the end they opted for Bernie. That was fine with me – Bernie and I go back ten years and he was magnificent for me throughout the Tour.

I made my intentions clear as to who I wanted around me, my key figures. There were seven of them – the core group of riders who had been with me all season.

MICK ROGERS, thirty-one years old, was to be the team captain on the road. The tall and studious-looking Australian is a triple world time trial champion. He's a great team captain, very vocal, and in the 2012 Tour he called the shots on the road. He's the guy who judged the pace up the climbs, getting us to ride at what he felt was the right intensity, and he would calm us down when it began kicking off a bit and the others started attacking.

RICHIE PORTE was the other Aussie in the group. I didn't know him very well until he came to the team in 2011, although we'd raced the Giro together in 2010, when he won the young rider's jersey. Richie is a phenomenal climber, and a great time triallist as well.

KOSTA SIUTSOU said to Dave when he came to Sky, 'I just want to ride for the team – whatever you want me to do I'll do.' He's from Belarus, via Italy, and when we first met, he didn't speak a word of English. He likes his long five- or six-hour rides, and is an incredible bike rider in his own right – he's won a stage in the Giro, and finished top ten there; he's a former under-23 world champion, and he came sixteenth in the Tour in 2008.

CHRISTIAN KNEES is another with a great record; he finished in the top twenty in the Tour in 2009, which is quite a result for a big lad like him. He's a double German champion, another lovely guy, and he was phenomenal in the Tour. For the first five days he was constantly riding in the wind at the front of the race. He'd be on the side of the train leading the bunch, whichever team was riding, with me in his wheel keeping out of the wind. After five days of that we realized we simply had to give him a rest, but then we got to the first hilly stages and he was doing it again! Christian was the man of the match in the Tour.

Another contender for that title, though, is BERNHARD EISEL. Bernie is head of the lead-out train, Cav's right-hand man. He is the guy who will ride early on to make sure the sprint happens for Cav. However, Bernie is a hugely talented bike rider too, a very fast sprinter and one-day Classic star, who won Gent–Wevelgem in 2010.

Once we got into the 2012 Tour, as well as doing the job for Cav in the final kilometres of the sprint stages, Bernie had a presence when he was around that could make me feel special, like a million dollars. I could see why Cav loves him so much. It's hard to put your finger on it but, for example, on day one, we were riding to sign on in Liège and there were hordes of people trying to get there. He was behind me, but came past and said, 'I'll ride in front of you to make sure that you don't get knocked off your bike.' It's little things like that. Throughout the three weeks of the Tour, he was always in the same good spirits every morning, always smiling, always joking, never down about anything. He always knew what pace to ride, never panicked in any situation. In the first five or six days of the Tour when it was crazy at the front, he knew exactly where to ride to keep me out of trouble.

Although twenty-five-year-old Norwegian EDVALD BOASSON HAGEN wasn't racing with the climbing group all year, he was a rider we simply had to have with us in the Tour. I've been saying for years that Eddie is one of the most talented young bike riders of his generation, if not *the* most talented. He is capable of winning Classics, prologues and shortish time trials; he can get wins in bunch sprints like he did at the 2011 Tour in Lisieux and he can land stages from a break as he did in the last week of that Tour. On top of all that he can climb with the best of them in the mountains.

The team had learned their lesson since my broken collarbone in the Tour the previous year, so CHRIS FROOME was there as back-up after his second place in the Vuelta; he would step up only in an extreme case – basically, if I crashed out. Chris came to road cycling late, but that lack of experience is also his strength, because he has absolutely no fear – he's not intimidated by anyone.

The group had been handpicked over a couple of years to get to the point we were at in 2012.

It's like forming a soccer team – it takes time to buy in the players you need. But I can't say enough about the quality of what we called the climbing group within Sky; it consisted of guys who on their day were all potentially capable of challenging for a place on the podium in the Tour de France. Mick's finished top ten in the Tour and top ten in the Giro, Richie's run top ten in the Giro, Kosta as well, while Froomie had that second place in the Vuelta, and maybe could have won it. All of these riders were superbly talented, which helps explain why we were so dominant in the mountains.

The climbing group's performance in the Dauphiné had highlighted the team's strength, but what it didn't reveal was the depth of the commitment they showed for the whole nine months, right up to the end of the Tour. Riders like Mick, Kosta, Christian and Richie in particular, as well as Froomie, had totally bought in to what I was trying to do, to win the Tour in 2012. On top of their work in the races, they accepted that trying to win the Tour meant they had to sacrifice practically their entire season as a result, just to do that for me. That was a massive commitment from those guys and it's something I will never forget. It's kind of humbling too, to think that they all did that for me. You cannot forget that those guys are capable of winning races themselves and I'll be for ever grateful for what they did. Just saying thank you isn't enough; that's the way I feel about it.

Sean Yates – a working-class hero
Sean has been the lead *directeur sportif* at Sky since midway through 2010 but he and I go back a long, long way.

Sean Yates, a working-class hero. When he'd been racing, he was someone the British cycling public could associate with – he'd come from where they were, their world of club time trials and winter runs.

Sean hasn't changed through all those years. He's still the same as a *directeur sportif* as he was when he was a rider. He was legendary as one of the hard men of the sport, but if someone's pulled out of a race because they've got cold or it was too hard, he'll never say, 'Oh, when I was riding, I would never have done that.' He's always sympathetic. He'll say, 'OK, you know how you feel.'

It's a big job being a *directeur sportif*; in the old days the DS ran everything at a team, from budgets to training and tactics. Now, mainly, a DS has to plan the tactics beforehand, make sure the riders are fully supported while the race is on – that means keeping them fed and watered on the move – and figure out the tactics on the hoof as the race unfolds.

Sean is the best DS I've ever had. He's unbelievable. He shows as much attention to detail in what he does as we do in what we're doing on the bike. He's capable of doing everything at once: driving the car, talking to us on the radio, talking to someone else on the phone, handing out bottles and gels as the guys come back for them. In a time trial he has a list of things you're coming up to – he's got it all written down: 'Descending through a village, there's a sharp right-hander, eighty, a hundred metres to go before this village there's a slight pothole on the left.' He's like a vocal GPS system for the riders.

As a DS, he's just completely on the ball. There are times when crucial decisions need to be made on the road – such as, *Shall we ride behind a break or not?* – and there might be a disagreement. At times like this, Sean will make the call. It's never about him. There was one occasion I saw a while back in a race, where he made the snap decision not to stop for a rider after a puncture; Sean felt he needed to be up the road with the front group as soon as possible because we had a rider there who looked good for the overall, but who had no support. He took a lot of flak from the one who had punctured, because the rider felt he could have won the stage, but in the meeting Sean stood up and said, 'I know you're annoyed with me but I did what I thought I had to do at the time. You're going to have to deal with that, and you can continue to be annoyed, but I made a decision at the time in the middle of all this madness and I think I did the right thing.' Where a lot of people would have apologized, he didn't give a monkey's whether the rider liked him or not. He just wanted to do his job for the team. It was time to move on.

Sean never tries to push himself forward; he never does what some former riders do, which is to tell you how good they were in their day. He tells his stories and he's clearly proud of what he did, but he doesn't try to put himself in the limelight. When he does his job he just wants to see the riders succeed. All he asks of people as a *directeur sportif* is 100 per cent commitment, to give their all, and as long as they do that he's happy. As we went into the mayhem of the Tour de France, it was Sean who would be guiding us from the Team Sky support car. And I wouldn't have asked for anybody else in that front scat.

The particular feeling of confidence I have had in my best years is a hard thing to explain – it's not confidence that you are unbeatable but confidence that you have done the work to the maximum of your ability, and all you have to do now is empty the tank, be the best athlete you can, and accept what you get from it at the end. I knew I had done the work. Going into a race knowing you've got the form is completely different from when you don't know and you're just hoping you're going to do well.

That sense I had that things were going my way was reinforced the moment I landed in Belgium to begin the Tour.

I'd done all that work.

I was fine-tuned.

Ready to go.

I took a private jet to Liège as an investment, making a point of paying for it myself because, having done everything I had done, I didn't want to get a low-cost flight and spend half a day travelling. So I went out training that Wednesday, did my fine-tuning on the bike, then took a jet out of an airfield close to my home, straight to Belgium. The *soigneur* from Sky who collected me said, 'Cadel's just arrived.' He had flown in ten minutes before me, in his own jet as well, but no one from his team had been there to pick him up and he was getting really irate. We got straight in the car, drove past Cadel standing there with his bike next to him, and I started thinking, 'We're at the Tour, here we are.'

And I got the feeling the race had started on the wrong foot for Cadel, even if in a very, very small way.

BACK IN THE MADHOUSE

Seraing, 29 June 2012

The first 'proper' stage of the Tour has finished. I'm feeling furious as I climb off my bike at the top of the hill, hand it to the mechanic and climb into the bus. I'm raging. The insanity of the early stages of the Tour has been rammed home, and I have just been reminded it's not going to be easy.

I'm in the form of my life. All I've got to do is get to the open road and I can win this race. But I could lose all this because of some idiot; and I might never get this opportunity again . . .

It's a dogfight. I don't like that side of it.

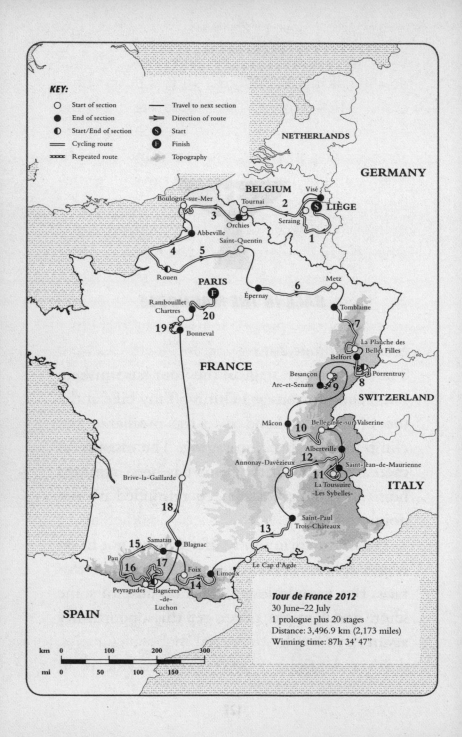

KEY:
○ Start of section
● End of section
◐ Start/End of section
═══ Cycling route
✕✕✕ Repeated route

── Travel to next section
⇒ Direction of route
Ⓢ Start
Ⓕ Finish
▨ Topography

NETHERLANDS

GERMANY

BELGIUM

Visé
Ⓢ LIÈGE

Boulogne-sur-Mer
Tournai
2
3
Orchies
Seraing
1
Abbeville
Saint-Quentin
4
5
Rouen
PARIS
Ⓕ
Métz
Rambouillet
Chartres
Épernay
6
Tomblaine
20
7
19
Bonneval
La Planche des
Belles Filles
Belfort
Porrentruy
FRANCE
Besançon
8
Arc-et-Senans
9
SWITZERLAND
Mâcon
10
Bellegarde-sur Valserine
Albertville
12
Annonay-Davézieux
Saint-Jean-de-Maurienne
Brive-la-Gaillarde
11
ITALY
La Toussuire
-Les Sybelles-
18
Saint-Paul
Trois-Châteaux
13
15
Samatan
Pau
Blagnac
16
17
Foix
Le Cap d'Agde
Peyragudes
Bagnères-
de-Luchon
14
Limoux
SPAIN

km   0   100   200   300
mi   0   50   100   150

Tour de France 2012
30 June–22 July
1 prologue plus 20 stages
Distance: 3,496.9 km (2,173 miles)
Winning time: 87h 34' 47"

I like having an open road and letting my legs do the talking. I could lose all this in one little crash. Mick Rogers was riding right behind me; someone rode into him with 20km to go and that was it; Mick lost four minutes. Your Tour could be over on day one through something as simple as that.

In the first week of the Tour there are times when it's an absolute lottery whether you crash or not, unless you are in the very front line of the peloton. That's why I was raging. Coming in as favourite, part of me thought the other riders would give me space. In other races we'd been given quite a bit of respect in the opening stages, so it was a bit of a shock on day one – you know what? Actually no one cares.

The opening phase of the Tour is always crazy, chaotic and nerve-racking, and the 2012 race was no exception. It's only like that at the Tour. It's never quite as hectic at other major races. My goal for the early part of the Tour was simply to get to the point where the way was clear in front of us. That meant either the stage finish at Planche des Belles Filles after seven days, or the time trial in Besançon nine days in.

So we were in for a week of mayhem.

For once, the waiting game for the couple of days before the prologue time trial wasn't too tense. I always room on my own when we have nine riders at a race, so I have my music and everything with me. I like being in my own space, just enjoying my own company. The night before the prologue I was sitting in my room listening to The Jam. John Dower, who was making a film about my year, asked me, 'How do you feel at the moment?' and I remember saying, 'I can't wait.' I was feeling 100 per cent confident and I was enjoying being favourite for the Tour. It might never happen again: it is the stuff of dreams.

Shoulder to shoulder in the first week

I was probably more relaxed than I've ever been going into the prologue, which took place over 6.4km in the centre of Liège. I knew I was the best over the distance out of the guys going for the overall, so it was almost a question of how much time I could take out of the others.

And I had the fastest time on the board for a while, until Fabian Cancellara came in and did better, but he wasn't expected to feature over the long-term as he struggles in the mountains. Critically, Cadel Evans ended up ten seconds behind me. The first skirmish was over and I'd gained time on all my main rivals!

With the other Sky riders packing well behind me — Eddie fifth, Froomie eleventh and Christian 26th — we were well placed in the team standings. That in turn meant our support car would be close to the front of the convoy — in the Tour, the order of the cars is decided by the team rankings — guaranteeing us quick service if we had any problems. It's a small thing, but they all count.

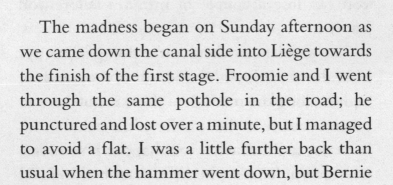

The average rider will wear out three chains over the course of the 23-day event.

The madness began on Sunday afternoon as we came down the canal side into Liège towards the finish of the first stage. Froomie and I went through the same pothole in the road; he punctured and lost over a minute, but I managed to avoid a flat. I was a little further back than usual when the hammer went down, but Bernie moved me up close to the front, and then I was able to work my way up the outside once we all started going up the hill to the finish. Then I played it safe and stayed with Cadel.

There are various reasons why the first week of the Tour ends up the way it does. First up, there are two hundred bike riders wanting to ride at the front of the peloton. There's no significant hierarchy in the first week of the Tour, so everyone feels they've got a chance to win the stage or get in the break: no one team has control because the overall contenders haven't emerged.

Crashes are the main worry. Your Tour could be over in the first week, not just because you fall off and break something: if there's a crash in front of you and you can't get past it, you can lose a couple of minutes before you know it.

The problem is when you're doing 65km per hour down a hill with hundreds of thousands of people along the roadside – there is nowhere to go and you are in the middle of the peloton. It's hard not to think what will happen if someone goes down. That's when you start braking and drifting back, when you try to get to the side and move up. It's horrible. I don't mind admitting I'm scared at times when the race is like that. When a crash does happen, the first you know about it is when you are on the ground with a broken collarbone or something. It's not as if you see it coming. You don't have time to think about it; you react to it when it happens.

Over the last few years it's become apparent that the only way to avoid falling or getting held up is to ride on the front; that's what most teams try to do now. This is where you get the trains going, as a whole team lines out to make the pace with their protected rider or riders at the back of the string, and the peloton sheltering behind.

Riding in the trains is hard work on a team. There is a lot of concentration involved, and if you start doing it, other teams will take it up as well, because everyone starts panicking. Suddenly everyone wants to get to the front, because they sense something may be happening. That's when the craziness starts. As you get closer to the finish it gets worse and worse, to the point where something has to give and then there's a crash.

So all the guys who are going for the overall want to ride at the front of the bunch to keep out of trouble, and all their eight riders are trying to ride there to protect them. Straight away you've got forty or fifty riders in the front. Then you've got the sprinters' teams with their eight riders in there, so that's another forty guys. That makes nearly a hundred, or half the peloton, wanting to ride at the front. Imagine walking down Oxford Street in central London on the last weekend before Christmas at the height of the shopping period and how close you are to people there – that's how close we are. We are talking shoulder to shoulder, with no margin for error.

The crowds are one thing that make the Tour more stressful than other races. You've got more spectators than at any other race and they narrow the road even further – they've all got a phone or a digital camera or an iPad taking pictures of the race too, so their hands are protruding towards the peloton, and that's another few inches taken up, so it's difficult to move up the outside of the bunch. I think sometimes the fans don't realize how close to us they are and how fast we are moving. People

A DEADLY SPORT

There are many mountain climbs in the Tour de France. The hardest climb is the Mont Ventoux. In 1967, a British cyclist, Tom Simpson, died of exhaustion half a kilometre from the top of this mountain.

In total there have been four deaths since the beginning of the Tour de France. In 1995, an Italian rider, Fabio Casartelli, crashed at approximately 88 kph without wearing a helmet. In 1935, a Spanish rider, Francisco Cepedar, died after plunging into a ravine. The race itself wasn't always the cause of death at the Tour. In 1910, a French rider called Adolphe Helière drowned at the Riviera during one of the two rest days.

have got prams in the road – they jump back and leave the pram out there, or a guy in a wheelchair sitting in the road, or a tripod with their camera on it. It's just chaos. All the riders are trying to avoid crashing by being on the front so the peloton turns into an arrow head, racing along, with all that going on at the sides of it.

In the first week of the Tour, each day is different so there's no set pattern to the stages. Stage one had a hard uphill finish so all the guys going for the general classification were up there, plus all the climbers, as well as riders going for the stage. Stage two into Tournai, when Cav won, was calmer, because there are only certain sprinters who have a chance in that kind of finish, so at least in the final five kilometres the guys going for the overall tend to slip back a bit.

The sprinters get scared as well. I remember Cav and I talking about the sprints one day, and I said, 'Go on, you love it, don't you,' and he answered, 'I don't, that's just it, I hate it. I hate doing the sprints.' It looks so spectacular and thrilling, but he hates risking his life.

The first bad pile-up was on the Tuesday, coming into Boulogne; we were descending on a country road and they started falling at twentieth wheel from the front, and that was it. Bam. It blocked the road completely. I didn't think twice: I got off my bike, put it on my shoulder like a cyclo-cross rider, and ran down the verge into a field to get round as there was no way through all the guys on the deck. I had to do it – if you stand on the road you're going to wait there for a couple of minutes, and a lot of people didn't come back from that crash.

That ended up being one of my hardest days on the Tour. For a little while it felt like touch and go, as immediately after the crash I was the only rider from the team in the front group and I was thinking, 'I'd better not puncture here.' It was about 20km to go, and I'd never have got back in.

A rider will burn nearly 124,000 calories over the course of the Tour de France. That's as much as burning off approximately 1,000 baguettes!

DID YOU KNOW?

The other big problem was that I didn't take in enough food during the stage with all that was going on. Usually I eat as much as I can, constantly. I have a routine: every twenty minutes, eat something or take a gel. Rice cakes are what I tend to have with me – our chef Søren makes them, like rice pudding congealed into little squares.

But there was no time for that: even before the big crash, the stage had turned into a complete scramble. The crowds were huge, the roads were narrow, you couldn't move up for fear of hitting a spectator, there were small crashes going on so you were constantly chasing back to the bunch; with all that to think about, I kept forgetting to eat. I got really cold that day and I was struggling at the end. I had nothing left when we hit the finale. Without a doubt I would have lost time on Cadel Evans and the others on the climb to the finish. Luckily for me, however, I was caught behind yet another crash right at the end. I say lucky because it came inside the last 3km – the point after which they give you the same time as the lead group if you are held up in a crash. Losing five or ten seconds at that point would have been a huge blow.

The Boulogne crash was where we lost Kosta with a broken shin. I saw him in the hotel after the stage on Tuesday and the big picture was the last thing on my mind – you just feel so sorry for a guy who's broken his leg and will be healing for three months. We were dithering a bit at times in that first week, and as we went down into Rouen a crash happened with Cav. It was pretty horrendous – someone dropped a bottle as they were lining up for the sprint and he ended up with cuts and grazes all over.

The day after, Saint-Quentin, that was it, we

team time trialled for 25km and I gave a bit of a lead-out to Cav at the finish. On that stage, in fact, we were killing two birds with one stone: we were covering my backside against crashes but we were also keeping Cav up in the front for the sprint. We were all super-happy with ourselves after that day.

The crash that made the biggest impact in the first week was the 'massacre' on the way to Metz, which happened about 25km out from the finish and cost several contenders their chance in the race. We were doing 70km per hour down a long straight road, with the trains on the front of the bunch; apparently the crash was started by a guy who used to be in our team, Davide Viganò. His team leader, Alessandro Petacchi, decided to remove his overshoes – he took one off, gave it to Viganò, took the other one off and Viganò took his hands off the bars, sat up to put them in his back pocket, touched a wheel and that was it: *bang*, carnage.

Just before it happened, I was twenty riders back in the bunch, and I remember thinking, 'This is ridiculous, this is getting crazy.' The crowds were closing in on us from the sides of the roads. I thought: 'If there's a crash now, I'm down, there's nowhere to go.' Then I saw an opening and I went right up the outside with Christian Knees on my wheel; we passed the GreenEDGE train on the front and got in the slipstream of the motorbikes. We were doing 75km per hour behind a motorbike, so I stopped pedalling, looked round, put my hand out and apologized to GreenEDGE for overtaking them. That was just a matter of respect; telling them I wasn't showboating when they were riding at the front. At that point the crash happened behind me, right where I had been sitting. You think: 'Was that fate?' If I hadn't moved up that would have been my Tour over there and then.

I went through that Tour without a single puncture or crash. Was that luck? Or was that me being on the ball, completely focused and putting as much thought into every single stage as if it was the only one that counted, in a way that I hadn't done the year before? It made me think of something Chris Boardman said. He was asked to sum up what quality it is that makes me a strong Tour contender. He said, 'It's hard to put your finger on one thing, but as I've found out over the last ten years, the thing that makes Brad good is his ability to learn.'

I think that's quite a reasonable summary. My crash in 2011 was definitely a lesson. And think how many guys going for the overall got wiped out in that one crash at Metz – perhaps that was the day when I really won the Tour.

High up at La Planche des Belles Filles
After the Dauphiné, Sean and I had gone and looked at the stage finish at La Planche des Belles Filles, high up in the Vosges above the town of Nancy. In all the races we'd done up to that point it had become clear that the most efficient way for me to climb was just to ride as hard as possible at the bottom to put everyone in the red. Then I could ride what amounted to a time trial up to the top.

The goal for the stage was to hit the climb, 8.5km to the finish, with Mick on the front, then Richie, Froomie and me. It wasn't super-long so we would ride above threshold: very hard work. Mick would go as hard as he could, which would probably be a kilometre and a half, Richie would take over and do the same thing, then Froomie. Eventually we would get to the summit and there shouldn't be many other guys left with us.

Planning a finish like this is just a matter of working back in stages from the goal and figuring out who does what in each section. We'll agree that the way we need to do it is to keep Mick, Richie, Froomie and Brad for the summit; we'll say, 'Eddie it's your job to take it up from that last climb and do the descent, Christian, you're on bottle duty all day and if you can pace the guys going into that second last climb your job is done, Bernie, go as far as you can, Cav, you're on bottle duty as well,' and that's it.

So that was the goal at La Planche des Belles Filles – it was then a question of getting into the right position. Before the final ascent, there was a climb that dragged up for a while, followed by quite a nasty, fast little descent. We knew we needed to be in the front for that descent, and the best man for that job would be Edvald. So working back from that, Christian and Bernie could do the job to get us there early on. We decided that 500m from the summit we were going to hit the front with Eddie, and he was

140

going to go full on down the descent, take it to the foot of the climb, with the peloton in one line. Then Mick would take over, followed by the three of us.

And that's exactly what happened.

While all that was going on in the race, I just sat there in the line. When we actually hit that climb to La Planche des Belles Filles, Mick was doing his thing and it was very hard, but you're composed and you think, 'Yeah, I can take this up a level, it's not a problem.' Then you get a kilometre, two kilometres into the climb, Richie takes over, two and a half, three kilometres into the climb, you're halfway up, Richie's on the front, you're working hard, and you're thinking, 'I'm still in control of everything, I'm nowhere near getting dropped.'

Going up there, with the pace we were setting, no one was going to attack. At the end, bizarrely, Cadel tried to get away but I didn't know why he did that. He pressed on through a little flat bit, took the corner first into the last steep part of the climb, then just stopped. It was really weird and showed he didn't have the legs straight away. Then, on that final ramp,

Froomie pulled away in the final metres to win the stage.

We had done the job.

When I pulled on the yellow jersey a little while later it felt as if nothing else mattered. Regardless of what might happen in the rest of that Tour de France, I'd taken the yellow jersey! Overall leader at this point! Wearing the *maillot jaune* had been my dream from when I was about ten or twelve, so to achieve it was something that's hard to put into words. To join the handful of Britons who have worn yellow – Tom Simpson, Chris Boardman, Sean Yates, David Millar – was a big moment and I knew what it meant. I phoned Cath, phoned my mum; there's not a lot to say other than 'Did you watch it?'

I'd never had a yellow jersey in my hands; I'd never been in a team that took the jersey. Whatever happened in the rest of the Tour, I'd taken the yellow jersey in the Tour de France. I'd be able to say that for the rest of my life when going down to the café on my bike: '*I took the yellow jersey in the Tour.*'

Cycling is a unique sport. It's the only one where this idea exists – that it's an achievement in itself to take the race lead in the biggest event even just for a day. Wearing yellow in the Tour is not like leading the Premiership, or being in front at the Masters for a day, or first man in the London Marathon at the five-mile point. I remember watching Sean take it in 1994 at Rennes, when he held it for only one day. I was fourteen, seeing just what it meant, not even winning the yellow jersey at the end of the Tour, but just wearing it for one day. You get to keep it for the rest of your life too. You can put it in a picture frame or whatever you choose to do with it to remind you: *I held the yellow jersey in the Tour de France.*

IN THE FIRING LINE

Wearing the yellow jersey

My first stage in the yellow jersey was a hard day into Switzerland, up and down constantly, finishing at the little town of Porrentruy. Physically, it included the hardest point of the whole Tour for me. It was a short day, just under 160km, so the race was on from the off, but the support I had from the boys was unbelievable, particularly Christian Knees.

There were only five or six of us left over the top on the last climb – a short steep one. I felt I was close to getting dropped off the group towards the end. But I was riding a super-light bike and a few days later I realized that it had cracked under the bottom bracket so it was flexing like crazy and that's why I was finding it so hard. But that's the point about the Tour – the race is never done and dusted. Something can always happen. We had a healthy scrap into the finish, Van Den Broeck and Cadel attacking, me chasing them down quite comfortably. It was like being a junior again, racing for the hell of it.

With that Swiss stage over, I began thinking about the next key day: the Besançon time trial. I just wanted to get back to the hotel and get on with preparing for it – I didn't want to stick around at the finish doing all the press interviews. But as the yellow jersey of the Tour de France, you have no option.

DID YOU KNOW?

In the Tour de France, you tour more than France. While most stages of the Tour are in mainland France, since the 1960s stages have been held in Andorra, Belgium, England, Germany, Ireland, Italy, Luxembourg, Monaco, the Netherlands, Spain and Switzerland. In 2012, the route passed through Belgium and Switzerland.

The doping question
The doping talk about me on Twitter had

begun after the Tour of Romandie, and they had continued after Sky had dominated at the Dauphiné. So I'd been thinking about what to say for some time. I don't often lose my temper, but this had made me angry. And I knew that if I went well at the Tour the accusations were going to happen more and more. I was waiting for it and had decided that when the question was asked I was just going to give them the kind of answer they'd expect if they asked me in the pub.

When asked about the comments on the Net, I was very direct. With a lot of bad language! I told the press: 'I cannot be doing with people like that. It justifies their own bone-idleness because they can't ever imagine applying themselves to doing anything in their lives.' And more . . .

With that, I got up and left the caravan where we do the written press after the stage. There was, I'm told, a small ripple of applause back at the main press room, and for some people that statement has become a bit of a John Lennon moment. Someone came up to me recently, with some great big yellow posters printed out with that quote on it, then a little dash and my name. I signed them; in years to come, maybe you'll see that answer in a book of proverbs, signed Bradley Wiggins!

I wanted to nip the accusations in the bud straight away. I just went for it, and I don't see why I shouldn't be allowed to do that. Even if we are athletes in a public position, we are also human beings. I've always tried to be genuine, and I will continue to be. That didn't have to change just because I was trying to win the Tour.

I don't want to be cast in the role of a moral hero though. Back in 2006 and 2007, there seemed to be an idea that I was spearheading a massive campaign for anti-doping. *Cycle Sport* did a piece in 2006 with me on the front cover headlined: THE WHISTLEBLOWER. I was happy to talk about it but that wasn't how I wanted to be seen. Just because I've given my opinion on something doesn't mean that I want my views to be seen as the opinion of a group or a nation. I don't see myself as a leader in that sense, or a campaigner.

When I turned professional, I was of course aware of what might be going on. I didn't see anyone doping – using specific drugs to enhance their performance – but suspected people were dabbling in lesser stuff. You're quite easily influenced when you are young – one way I look at it is it's like the pressure there is to smoke when you're a teenager. But I was lucky: I got together with Cath in 2002 and based myself in Manchester. It meant I ended up some distance away from European cycling, where a rider could dope, be caught, be banned and still come back and be a national hero.

I get incredibly angry when I'm accused now of doping, or even when it's merely implied. That accusation is like saying to someone else: you cheat at your job; you cheated to get to where you are now. I can understand why I was asked about doping at the Tour, given the recent history of the sport, but it still annoyed me. There is plenty I've said in the past that should make it clear where I stand.

It is only now that we have a much clearer idea of what was going on in the sport some time ago. After 2006 and 2007, the drugs tests began to work more efficiently, the blood passport came in and it got harder for people to dope. The important thing is that nothing has changed in where I stand. The question that should be asked isn't: *Why wouldn't I take drugs?* But: *Why would I?*

I know exactly why I wouldn't ever dope. If I did I could lose everything. And it's a long list. My reputation, my livelihood, my marriage, my family, my house. Everything I have achieved, my Olympic medals, my world titles, the CBE I was given. I would have to take my children to the school gates in a small Lancashire village with everyone looking at me, knowing I had cheated, knowing I had, perhaps, won the Tour de France, but only because I had cheated.

And it's not just about me. All my friends in cycling are here, and my extended family. Cycling isn't just about me and the Tour de France. My wife organizes races in Lancashire, and I have my own *sportif*, with people coming and paying £40 each to ride. If all that was built on sand, if I was deceiving all those people by doping, it could disappear just like that. Who would risk that?

I race bikes because I love it, and I love doing my best and working hard. I don't do it for a power trip. At the end of the day, I'm a shy bloke looking forward to taking my son rugby training after the Tour, perhaps bumping into my lad's hero, Sam Tomkins. If I felt I had to take drugs, I would rather stop tomorrow, go and ride club ten-mile time trials, ride to the café on Sundays, and work in Tesco stacking shelves.

It came out during the 2012 Vuelta that Lance Armstrong was being stripped of his titles. I haven't followed all the ins and outs of his case, but I know that he's not contesting the doping charges against him (although he's still protesting his innocence); as it stands his Tour titles have been taken away from him and it seems clear that he was doping in a sophisticated way. I do know that if it were confirmed that he was doping in 2009–10, then there is nothing he could say in his defence – he would have let the whole sport down. Before then, he wouldn't have been alone in what he was doing, but the sport has changed since he retired the first time.

THE OTHER TEAM

The morning of the time trial in Besançon was exactly the same as for any other time trial I've ever ridden. I was in the old, familiar routine, which I relish so much. But one thing sticks out. When we got to the start, I sat on the chair by the ramp and all the cameras came in front of me: *flash, flash, flash*. At that point I've got my eyes shut; I don't look at them. I just sit like that with my eyes closed under the visor but I can still see all those flashing things through my eyelids. I remember thinking, 'I wish they'd stop doing that', so I made a conscious mental note about it: when I got to Chartres eleven days later, and I went to the start, I would turn my chair round so that I could sit with my back to all the cameras.

The announcer introduced Cadel Evans, who was lying second overall and was the second-last rider off, three minutes in front of me: 'This is Cadel Evans, the winner of last year's Tour de France; he's second overall, only ten seconds behind Bradley Wiggins.' The crowd was getting hyped up, really hyped up, and eventually Cadel came down the ramp. There was that massive crowd noise you hear when a rider starts, and that noise was following him up the road. I was wearing a thin little jersey over my skinsuit; the second he started I unzipped it, took it off and threw it on the floor to show I was really ready. I slapped my hands together and went to the ramp.

Usually, when you have that long to wait before a time trial, you sit down below in the chair for two minutes then go up on to the start ramp; here, I was desperate to get into the start house on top of the ramp so that I could watch Cadel go. In that time trial there was about a 3km straight from the start before a left-hand bend; I went up the ramp at once, sideways on with my bike, and then I stood in the entrance to the start house, watching his car going down that straight. I rested my arms on my skis and I was just watching the car going further and further away. I was talking to myself: *'I'm coming after you. I'm coming after you.'*

Then they said, 'One minute to go,' so I rolled up, clicked into the pedals, got myself ready, watching Cadel's car all the time. It was still in sight, like a pinprick in the distance, and then it was suddenly gone. I heard the thirty-seconds-to-go call, and the announcer said, 'Bradley Wiggins, winner of the Dauphiné Libéré, Paris–Nice, Tour of Romandie . . .'

Ten seconds to go, the crowd were making a huge noise, and I could hear that count: *five, four, three . . .*

I pushed back, and straight away I was out hard for the first ten or twelve seconds, then down onto the saddle and into my pace.

And then Sean started the dialogue: 'OK, Brad, you know what you've got to do today: you've got three kilometres straight here, then you've got a left-hander, do what you do best.' So I settled down and it felt really good, really strong. We got out of the first 5km, then it was out on to a bigger, wider road that dragged up for about 1.5–2km. I remember Sean saying, 'You're twenty seconds ahead of Cadel.' It was after about 5km and I thought, 'What?' I hadn't even started pushing on at that point!

We went into a super-fast section, speeding round the sweeping bends, doing about 65km per hour. I put my head down and the visor flew off my helmet. It hadn't been stuck on properly; the magnet on the right-hand side had come undone, so it just whizzed off. And I had to deal with it. My eyes had got used to having the visor in front of them, so they started watering a lot in the wind. I was blinking continually at first but my eyes adapted. All that time the gap kept going up. All the checks until close to the end had been on Cadel. At 10km to go, Sean said: 'You've got one-nineteen on Cadel, and you're sixteen seconds ahead of Froomie; he's got the best time.' I had been just thinking about Cadel the whole time until then, but I suddenly thought, 'Wow, Froomie, sixteen seconds, that's a good ride from him.'

Towards the end, the course was flat for about 6km, then there was a left-hander, up a climb and Sean said, 'This is where you're going to make the difference.' I remember thinking,

'Forget Cadel, this is where I win the stage.'

I was motoring.

I remember taking the effort up another level through the flat section, and then I had to empty it on the last climb. In the end I took 1min 43sec on Cadel, but the thing that struck me most when I finished was that I'd won a stage in the Tour de France. A couple of days before I had been thinking, 'I've taken the yellow jersey in the Tour de France' – now I had won a stage! And I had 1min 53sec overall lead on Cadel and 2min 05sec on Froomie. We were nine days in – and I had got the best part of two minutes' lead on my main rival . . .

Home support
On the Tour you become institutionalized. You do the same thing day in, day out, as a matter of routine for the best part of four weeks – the race is over three weeks, but you're there several days before it starts – and you only ever see the same people around you. Apart from the fans and the media who follow the race, you almost forget what's going on in the outside world. I don't know how it feels to be behind bars, but seeing Cath on the rest day of the Tour de France

always makes me wonder if this is what it's like getting a visitor when you're in prison.

I'm not sure my wife Cath knew what to make of it either, being catapulted into the middle of the Tour for about twenty-four hours. From my point of view, it's just nice when you've been in the thick of it for two weeks to have someone come in from the outside to talk about some things other than cycling. It's a reality check – a rapid glance into the world back home, bits and pieces that were going on before you went to the Tour, that you've almost forgotten about. Cath's visit was brief; she was off home the next day. But seeing her was vital; throughout the whole of 2012 she's been the one who is always there – and she's been there for me for ten years.

We've known each other since I was about fifteen and we were on the junior national squad together. She's seen me through the good times, the bad times, the ups, the downs and the great times. Since we got together in 2002 we've been a team. The little things that she helps me with are as much a part of the big picture as the training and the planning I do with Shane and Tim. The difference is that

Shane goes home every day, and Tim goes home every day, but Cath comes home every day with me. It's a very hard, very selfish life that I live, and Cath and our children – Ben and Isabella – are completely there with me.

Cath knows when I am on it, not on it, skiving, not skiving, or when I'm making excuses. She knows me better than anyone – and is also my biggest fan. I cannot say this often enough or loudly enough: when it comes to winning Olympic gold medals and yellow jerseys, there is as much sacrifice from my family as there is from me, if not more. I wasn't home much in 2012 – I think it was five weeks between 1 January and 1 August.

Two weeks before the Tour we all got together in Majorca, but I was training, obviously, four, five, six hours of the day, so it's not as if we all go down the beach. I'd have a split day – a time trial in the morning, time trial in the evening – and I'd come back in between and have food and a sleep. We'd nip down the beach together at lunchtime and I'd have a coffee, but I'd have to sit in the shade. Cath and the kids would be outside; they'd all be on the beach and they'd run up and say, 'Come on, come in the sea with us, come on the lilo,' and I would have to say, 'I can't, I've got to stay here. I've got to go out training again later.'

Where Cath and the kids have made a difference is in their willingness to give things up for me, enabling me to live the way you have to if you are riding for the overall in the Tour.

In full training for the 2012 Tour de France, Brad consumed 7,000 calories a day, though burned up to 8,000 daily. He also gave up chocolate.

It can seem extreme, but there's thinking behind everything I do. I try never to walk any further than I have to, for instance. And my diet is just a constant daily thing. I fill up only as much as is absolutely necessary. That's the principle I live by. As Shane is always saying, 'It's like driving a car – you don't put fuel in it if you're not driving it.' It doesn't mean weighing my food. It's not quite as bad as that – you have to avoid getting into that obsessive stage where you're weighing your food and you're saying,

'Oh, I can't have a boiled sweet because that might affect me.' There is a bit of balance and a lot of common sense with everything and it is, of course, always important to have a healthy diet.

Living the way I do involves a whole lot of other little things, such as not putting my own suitcase into the car when I go to the airport before a race, and not taking my suitcase out of the car coming back. Cath does all that. She won't let me pick stuff up. The thinking is this: it just seems funny how you do all this training, all this preparation, all this work, all the fine-tuning for a race, and then, with two days to go, you've got to lift a twenty-five-kg suitcase in and out of the back of your car, lug it around an airport, take it off the conveyer belt and chuck it in the back of the taxi. You could do yourself an injury, and all that work would be for nothing. To me, not lifting the luggage is a part of the race. I almost take it for granted now. When I had finished at the Olympics and we were loading up the car to come back, I was waiting for Cath to put the cases in as usual and she said I could do it for myself now: 'Come on, you haven't got that excuse any more.'

The problem is that when I am at home, the UK isn't ideal for specific training to win the Tour de France, so I only really go home to rest and ride my bike. Then there comes a point where I have to go away and train again. That's the biggest sacrifice with Cath, Isabella and Ben: being out of their lives, missing their birthdays. But they all realize why I'm doing it, and the reward for doing something like this is worth the sacrifice. Cath and I are both in it together. It's teamwork and she has been happy for me to do it, for ten years.

But I'm not going to do it for ever.

It's now or never.

UNDER ATTACK

It was a really satisfying rest day in spite of the fatigue after the time trial the day before. I was really pleased to have a day off; we had a few moments to chill out and briefly savour the stage wins and the yellow jersey. It was as if the first part of the race was over.

You can't sit there, though, and just think about what you've won already. As well as relaxing, there was also a sense of making sure I did all the little things right, paying attention to those details: 'OK, what are we doing tomorrow? Ten o'clock on the bikes; plan the route.' That's how the Tour functions; you have to constantly look ahead. The next obstacle was made up of a pair of Alpine stages. The first, to Bellegarde-sur-Valserine, took us over the Col du Grand Colombier, super-steep in places but, as it turned out, a climb where the problem was less the *ascent* than the *descent*.

The following day, over the Col de la Madeleine and the Glandon/Croix de Fer en route to La Toussuire, the race took a more worrying turn, with Cadel making his most serious attack of the whole three weeks. It was a long-range move, and clearly had been planned. Cadel went for it on the Glandon with 75km to go, maybe 10km from the top, on quite a steep section before you turn on to the Col du Croix de Fer. It looked as if he'd attacked from quite a long way back in the group because when he came past us he wasn't accelerating, he was in full flight, as if he was sprinting for a finish line 400m away.

We had felt in control for most of the stage already, with Eddie doing a fantastic job over the Madeleine, and when Cadel put his foot down we were setting quite a decent tempo. We were determined not to panic, but just kept riding at our own rate. When you are riding at that kind of rhythm, not far off the limit, if someone is going to attack on a mountain and sustain it to the summit, they have to be extremely good to get away, let alone to open a decent gap. We were conscious that there was still a long way to go – down the Croix de Fer, up another ramp to the Col du Mollard, a second category climb, another descent to Saint-Jean-de-Maurienne, then a 17km climb to the finish.

So we slowly reeled in Cadel about a couple of kilometres before the summit of the Croix de Fer; you could see he was struggling. At that point, if we'd just turned it up a notch he would have gone, but I knew then that was it, he would not be able to back it up on La Toussuire when we got up there.

That was exactly what happened: he dropped almost 90sec and slipped to fourth overall. Later that day he said to me, 'Hats off to you guys today.'

Most of the stage to La Toussuire was a simple matter of attack and defence. Cadel threw down the gauntlet; we picked it up and threw it back. The rest wasn't so straight-forward.

We had a plan: control the race all day, then make the pace and do the peel-offs on the last climb.

Mick did an incredible job that day; he had

already worked a fair bit on the Glandon when Cadel made his move, but when he hit the foot of La Toussuire he rode for the first kilometre and a half; then he was done for the day. Next, Richie took over; he did 5km or so, he peeled off, and then Nibali attacked. Because Richie was done there was only one rider left to take over and that was Froomie, so he took up the job of setting the pace. He brought back Nibali's first attack and then, once he'd got him back, he stopped riding.

I assumed that he was finished, that the effort had taken its toll on him, but he kept pressing on for a little bit more and then Nibali attacked again, over the top of him, with Van Den Broeck taking it up with him. At this point Chris really slowed down, so I took it up. We had less than 10km to go, and I thought, 'Right, now I'm really going to have to pace this if I'm going to ride all the way to the summit on my own.'

I heard almost nothing through the radio earpiece. All I was getting was bits and bobs, because of the crowd making so much noise around us. So I started riding hard, in time-trial mode; I'd been on the front for about 2km, then we went up again as the road steepened coming into the village of Toussuire, just on the outskirts. At that point, Chris came hurtling past me, using the speed from going into the dip. He went straight to the front and said, 'Come on, let's go.' I jumped on his wheel; he lifted the tempo quite a bit. I'd already been pushing hard for 2km, so his initial acceleration put me in the red slightly. I hung on to him and shouted at him to back off: 'Whoa, Chris, whoa.'

But Froomie began pushing on a bit more, and when we got on to the back of the Nibali group, he attacked again and I just thought, 'I'm not going to put myself even more in the red so I'll just ride at my own tempo.' Chris was doing his own thing; I let him go and he attacked through the group.

There was a lot of confusion – it was a bit like having a battle plan going into a war, all being in a trench together, firing your guns at the enemy, and then one of your troops going off and doing his own thing somewhere else in another trench, completely unprompted, un-planned, and contrary to your original plan. I don't like uncertainty. I don't like to wonder:

'Are we doing it for him? What's the decision here?' I had said that we could ride for Froomie; if that was the case, just let me know either way. But we needed to make up our minds.

In pretty much everything I do, I like to have a plan, a tactic. It's very structured. If Nibali attacks, I'm expecting that, that's not a surprise; Nibali and the rest are rivals, so we all know it's going to happen. It's a team sport and we're going into war as a team, but all of a sudden my own teammate's attacking – and he's attacking not necessarily to get ahead of me but to put time into Nibali so he can move into second. That shouldn't be to the detriment of the job we're trying to do for me.

I think Chris got carried away in the heat of the moment. He was moving into second overall in the Tour de France; he was probably the best climber in the race. But I'd put my head on the block from the start of the season, saying I wanted to win the Tour de France. It was there; I was doing it. And we had set off with the plan in Liège: *'Brad's a dead cert for this race, he's proven it, you guys are all here to support him; but if Brad crashes out, Froomie, you're there as back-up.'* Everyone agreed to that. Everyone had signed up to that.

One thing is certain: Chris is a better climber than me, that's for sure. He's a more natural climber than I am and he's lighter than me, but on both those mountaintop finishes, I was leading the race by two minutes, so why risk all that?

The problem was that, from that moment on, through the rest of the Tour, I didn't quite know what to expect from Chris when it got into the heat of battle. I became very wary.

Being on the Tour is a bit like being in the *Big Brother* house; you forget after a while that the cameras are watching you. For those three and a half weeks, everything you do when the live television coverage is on is analysed; everything you say before and after the stage is examined. Everyone who follows the race is interpreting whatever you say in a good way or a bad way.

Because I was the one who had the yellow jersey and had to go into the mixed zone and face the microphones, it came down to me to answer all the questions at the finish: 'What was Chris Froome doing today?' It felt as if Chris was doing his own thing but I had to deal with it because as the race leader I was the one who was up for scrutiny in front of the press and television every day.

The questions I was asking myself about Froomie, and the questions I was being asked each day after the stage finished, certainly didn't make the Tour enjoyable. On top of the constant pressure to remain focused at every minute of every day, those external things made it much more stressful than it could have been or should have been. It was only at the very end that the race became something to treasure.

LIFE IN YELLOW

Every day when you lead the Tour you are given several *maillots jaunes*. There's a presentation one, which you receive on the podium in the evening, which is long-sleeved, with a zip up the back. The next morning you are issued with a bag containing the yellow kit for the race: one short-sleeved, one long-sleeved, one rain jacket and one gilet. Every day from La Planche des Belles Filles onwards, I folded up the ones from the podium and put them into my suitcase; the race jerseys might end up a bit shredded and dirty and would get washed; at the end of the race I signed a lot of them and gave them to the mechanics and *soigneurs* who'd helped me win them. I took one off at the finish at Luchon and gave it to a little British kid I saw. It still had the numbers on it; I said, 'Sorry about the smell, but if you still want it . . .' and threw it over to him.

The only ones I've kept are the short-sleeved yellow jersey I wore on my first day in yellow, with the numbers on – I put it in a plastic bag and it's hanging in my spare bedroom – the yellow jersey from Paris with the number on, and the presentation one from Paris. Those are the ones that mean the most.

It felt a bit bizarre the first day I was presented with the yellow jersey because it is something that you are so used to watching on the television; that famous music, the tune they always use for the podium. And the podium itself is like no other, a huge, huge thing. You go up there; Daniel Mangeas – the speaker who announces all the riders – is presenting you. Bernard Hinault zips up the jersey as you pull it on, which is strange – shaking the hand of one of the all-time greats, a five-time winner of the Tour.

On the road, being in yellow meant that overnight the race took on a structure. As the

BERNARD HINAULT

Nicknamed 'the Badger', Bernard Hinault is a former French cyclist known for five victories in the Tour de France. His wins in 1978, 1979, 1981, 1982 and 1985 have made him a Tour de France legend. Hinault is one of only five cyclists to have won all three Grand Tours, and the only cyclist to have won each more than once.

NATIONALITY French

BORN 1954

RIDER TYPE All-rounder

team with the jersey, suddenly Sky had the right to ride on the front of the race, which meant that a lot of the fighting within the peloton would fall by the wayside; immediately, the racing became more controlled. Overnight I had become the **patron** of the bunch, the more so because I had started the race as the favourite. There was no sense that I was just keeping the *maillot jaune* warm for someone else to take it later on in the race. I was the person everyone expected to be in that position. From that point onwards I had an open road.

That left us all in a completely different world compared to the chaos of the first week. Everything had changed. Sky were being shown respect on run-ins to bunch sprints – everyone was giving us that extra little bit of space on the road. If I stopped for a pee the whole race would seem to stop as well, because every rider knows there is no way anyone is going to attack when the *maillot jaune* has stopped – that's one of the unwritten rules of the peloton. If I went back to the car because I wanted to talk to Sean, everyone would think I'd got a mechanical, and again, no one would attack. But holding the yellow jersey from nearly two weeks out from the finish in Paris was something that no cyclist had managed since Bernard Hinault in 1981. It would be a mammoth task, and it would throw up situations that I had hardly expected.

A team usually decides together when to take a toilet break. There is an unwritten rule that riders do not attack when someone is answering a call of nature.

On the stages that took the Tour from the Alps towards the Pyrenees, the team moved into a daily routine that would look familiar to anyone who watches the big Tours. Firstly, a break would establish itself early in the stage, and we would decide how much of a margin it should be given. Sometimes there would be a long, intense period of attacking as one team or another tried to get riders in the move of the day; sometimes the move would go in the twinkling of an eye.

For those who wonder when they see me or another team leader sitting in the line behind their teammates, it's easier there, but not that easy. It's harder than sitting fifty or sixty back in the bunch, because you get more shelter when you are hidden deep in the peloton, but you can't account for the mental stress of being back there, and the mental strain adds to the physical demands.

What you can't calculate is the stress of leading a bike race. When I led the Dauphiné for just five days in 2011 I was mentally exhausted at the end because it was a new thing for me and it was a massive deal. I'm glad I came to the Tour with all those days leading smaller events behind me – everything at the Tour is on such a huge scale that if I'd led it for two weeks in 2011 I don't think I would have coped.

Tacks on the track

David Millar won the stage out of the Alps to Annonay, and the next day I did my best to lead out Eddie for what could have been a stage win in the bunch sprint.

But the biggest drama in the Pyrenees came on what had looked to be a relatively quiet stage into the little town of Foix, on what is now infamous as 'the day of the tacks', when someone – we still don't know who – tried to sabotage the race. There was one major climb on that stage, the Mur de Péguère, a steep, narrow one, ranked first category, but I remember feeling really good going up there. Close to the top, I went to the front of the group because it was getting quite narrow among all the spectators, and Sean told us to get bottles from the helpers the team had sent to wait at the top, because the cars were a fair way behind. I saw Rod standing by the road with a bottle, and swung over to the right-hand side to grab it; the other Sky riders did the same, and by all accounts most of the tacks had been dropped on the left, so we all missed them. We went over the top and thought, 'It's downhill all the way to the finish so that's the stage done now.'

The next thing I heard was Sean saying over the radio that a lot of guys seemed to have punctured. What followed was just chaos. About fifteen guys had punctured all at once: Cadel, Frank Schleck, all those guys . . . I knew something had happened, so I went to the front and told our boys to stop and shut it down – there was no point racing if everyone had punctured. Slowing everyone down to wait for the guys who'd punctured seemed the right thing to do. There's no point in trying to gain time from someone else's misfortune.

People read quite a lot into the way I acted. It was said that stopping the field at a time like that showed that I was behaving like the new *patron* of the peloton. It's not quite that simple. You just do what you do instinctively at the time. And then you get to the finish and find that all of a sudden your actions have kind of taken on a life of their own.

DID YOU KNOW?

The history of Tour de France is filled with occasions of sportsmanship. The French nicknamed Bradley Wiggins 'Le Gentleman' when he slowed to allow other racers to repair their bikes and catch up after saboteurs had thrown tacks on the road.

Meeting a childhood hero

There was one little event to savour when we reached the final rest day in Pau, with only three more days of racing before that final time trial. I had mentioned in an interview on the day I took the yellow jersey that I remembered watching the Tour as a kid and had never envisaged that one day I'd be taking the jersey; I said in that interview that my childhood hero in the Tour de France was Miguel Indurain, because he won every Tour from when I was eleven to the age of fifteen. It was the most influential period of my teenage years, and Indurain was the mainstay.

It must have got back to him somehow, and so on the rest day in Pau, Spanish television came to us and said, 'We want to do a piece with Brad, we've got something quite special for him.' They said it was from Indurain – a message from him, on the television screen; they translated it to me and it was basically him saying, 'Hello, Brad, I heard that you were a fan of mine, I think you're strong in the time trials like me,' and various other things. I was honoured just to think that he knew who I was; they said, 'He's also sent you this.' They gave me an envelope with a red scarf in it, one of the ones that they wear during the bull run in Pamplona. This particular one was a very sacred thing, with his family emblem on it. They explained: you can't buy it in the shops and it's a massive honour that he's given it to you. He'd signed it 'To my friend Bradley.' It was recognition from someone who had been my childhood idol – something that I simply

MIGUEL INDURAIN

Known as 'Miguelón' or 'Big Man', Indurain famously won five consecutive Tours de France from 1991 to 1995. He also won the Giro d'Italia twice, in 1992 and 1993, making him the dominant Grand Tour rider in the 1990s. As icing on the cake, Indurain won the first ever Olympic time trial in 1996.

NATIONALITY Spanish

BORN 1964

HEIGHT 1.88m (6ft 2in)

WEIGHT 80kg (176lb)

RIDER TYPE All-rounder

hadn't expected, and it meant all the more for that.

All through this, my philosophy was to take it day by day. There's enough stress on the Tour without wondering how the other guys are doing, and worrying about who might do what, when and where. You can never assume anything.

There was a classic case of this with Vincenzo Nibali in 2012 on the run-in to Luchon – a long, brutal stage through the Pyrenees over four big cols: Aubisque, Tourmalet, Aspin and Peyresourde. Nibali was obviously trying to put us under pressure on that stage; we finished the stage, and assumed he'd try that again for sure, because it had been tough.

On the next stage – the last one in the Pyrenees – Nibali put his boys on the front on the first big climb, Port de Balès; they made it hard there and lost some riders. So I sat behind Nibali the whole way up the climb and, towards the top of it, I got a sense of his body language, the way he was pedalling. I thought he might be struggling a little bit. I always watch people's pedalling action and I've learned that Nibali drops his heels when he's suffering. Now he started dropping his heels towards the top of the Port de Balès. His teammate Ivan Basso hit the front towards the summit, set quite a strong tempo and we descended off Port de Balès to climb the Peyresourde, the last major ascent of the whole Tour, with the finish at the top at the Peyragudes ski station.

Again Basso went to the front, again he set a really strong tempo, but about a kilometre and a half from the summit, the other riders started attacking and Nibali just couldn't respond. Straight away we realized he just hadn't backed up the efforts he'd made the day before. It was a classic case of expecting someone to do something because of how they looked the day before, when in actual fact they haven't got the legs for it.

When you are leading the Tour, there are hard decisions to be made. It's not always a nice business, and during that Tour I couldn't help feeling at times that Mark Cavendish deserved better than he got. Right from when he had been selected for the Tour in June, I think he had been very conscious of what people thought. From day one in Liège he had said in team

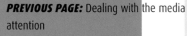

PREVIOUS PAGE: Dealing with the media attention

THIS PAGE:

Top left: Slogging it out on a training ride in Majorca

Left: The crowd giving me some encouragement!

Below: On my way to winning the 2012 Paris-Nice. It was that kind of year where everything just seemed to go right

FACING PAGE: I punch the air as I seal the Tour at Chartres!

THIS PAGE:

Top: Celebrating with the Sky team lads

Left: On the team bus after a race

Left: When I crossed the line on the Champs Élysées my first thought, as ever, was to seek out my wife Cath

Bottom: After winning the Tour de France everyone was looking at me, so I jumped on top of the team car!

PREVIOUS SPREAD:

Top left: Leading the Olympic road race up Box Hill with Froomie, David Millar, Ian Stannard and Cav on my wheel

Bottom left: Focused and raring to go at the Olympic time-trial start

Right: At the London 2012 Olympics

THIS PAGE: 'It was astounding; I am never going to experience anything like that again in my sporting life. Nothing is going to top that!'

meetings that he recognized that we were going for yellow and that he was determined to be part of it. His line was: 'I don't want to miss out on the opportunity to be in a British team going for the yellow jersey even if that means I'm not going to get a full lead out in the sprint.' It was difficult listening to him say that, and through-out the Tour, Cav was obviously keen to feel that he had played his part in trying to have a British Tour winner for the first time. That's why he was coming back for bottles on the stages when it wasn't going to be a sprint, and that's why on the first day in the Pyrenees he rode on the front most of the way up the climb of the Mur de Péguère – the day of the tacks and the punctures. All through the three and a half weeks, just having him around was a boost.

The day when I felt the most guilty about Cav was the day after he put that work in up Péguère; stage 15 into Pau. At just under 160km it was a short run and it was basically flat, but the break took 60km to get established. Until we let it go, we had some of the hardest racing of the whole Tour; constantly flat-out in one long line, with everyone's legs screaming.

When the break did eventually get away,

there was a feeling in the team that we should ride for Cav, out of respect for him and for the rainbow jersey. So we decided to put two guys on the front and start chasing a little. But as soon as Christian and Bernie had gone to the front, Mick Rogers came to me and said, 'This is wrong, I don't agree with it, we shouldn't be doing this.' Mick's thinking was that we'd been racing full-pelt for nearly an hour and a half and we didn't need to put our guys on the front. They'd already had some hard days in the mountains, and we had two big stages in the Pyrenees still to come. Something had to give. We couldn't chase everything, we couldn't treat our bodies as if they were indestructible; we could either roll along for the last 100km and get through the stage, or we could potentially ride our backsides off to bring this back for the sprint.

Eventually Mick went back to the car, and said to Sean: 'Look, this is the wrong decision, here, now.' Potentially he was risking the wrath of Cav, but the decision was made and Sean put the word out: 'OK, we're not going to ride. Stop riding, boys, that's it, Mick's right.' And that was that.

I remember talking to Cav on the road at the time; I could only say, 'Sorry, mate.' He was gutted that day because he really felt that he could win, but that was one of those situations where you have to play it safe.

We may have won the Tour that day because we saved two pairs of legs – Christian's for sure, and probably Bernie's. When we got into the Pyrenees after the rest day, it was Bernie who made the pace all the way up the Aubisque and along the valley, and Christian was able to ride a fair bit of the way up the Tourmalet. I take my hat off to Mick, because it takes a rider of huge experience and courage to make the call he did when he did, and particularly when you've got a sprinter of the quality of Mark Cavendish in the team. I wanted Mark to win but we had to be brutal at times and Mick took that decision.

In our attempt to win the yellow jersey, Mark was the rider within Sky who lost out the most. So that helps to explain what happened coming into Brive on the last Friday of the Tour. It was a long stage, 230km, up and down; the break went early and the peloton never seemed to be happy with it. It was the last chance for a lot of riders to win a stage and when it became clear

HOW A LEAD-OUT TRAIN WORKS

WIND DIRECTION

1: The team forms a line, with the sprinter at the back *(a)*. The rest of the team share the effort of pushing against the wind, allowing the sprinter to conserve energy by riding in the **slipstream**.

2: When the rider in front begins to get tired, they will hang back and swap places with one of the other riders. The sprinter remains at the back. By taking turns at being in front, the riders help each other to conserve energy.

4: Towards the last few hundred metres, the other riders gradually 'peel off' one by one, allowing the sprinter to burst to the finish line.

that a bunch kick was on the cards, I gave it everything in the final kilometre and a half to get Cav within reach of those last few **breakaways**.

I like the satisfaction you get from being part of a lead-out train, having that open road in front of you, doing your job, swinging off, watching someone like Cav win. It's a better feeling sometimes than winning yourself. But the time leading up to when you get in the position to do the lead out is the tough one.

BREAKAWAYS

During the race, a few riders will try to get ahead of the group and hold on to a lead to win the stage. The peloton will often try to chase this breakaway. Breakaways and chases can be very exciting to watch!

I knew that the following day I would have to go all out in the time trial and finish off the job of winning the Tour. But I had always wanted to be in yellow leading out the rainbow jersey for the sprint – it had been something I had thought about since the start of the Tour, and finally I had the chance to do it. I used the speed that I'd built up from that training on my core muscles, the little extra kick that had come through from the track, and pulled Cav until the final metres, when he produced one of the best sprints of his life to go past Luis León Sánchez and Nicolas Roche as if they were standing still.

That was four stage wins in the bag for Sky.

Just two more stages to go.

OPEN ROAD

Saturday 21 July 2012
Stage 19, 2012 Tour de France

It was nine months since the 2012 route had been confirmed with the long time trial on the last Saturday; in all that time I would never have imagined, or perhaps only in my wildest dreams, that I would go into that stage with a two-minute lead on my rivals.

It was during the stage before – the stage into Brive – that I started thinking about the time trial. And I began thinking, 'What if you can win the stage to seal the Tour?'

The stage to Brive was a long one; it turned

out to be actually quite a tough stage – we came into the finish and obviously we had a job to do for Cav. At that point there were no thoughts about the day after; it was just, 'Let's do this for Mark.' But once he'd won, my thoughts turned immediately to the time trial. I wanted to go back to the team bus to warm down properly and then we – the lead riders in the standings – had to get in helicopters to fly north for the time trial. Leading the race clearly took some of the pressure off. I wasn't trying to take the yellow jersey off another rider – I was defending it. But it wasn't a done deal.

At the start of a time trial in a professional race a lot of the riders roll out of the gate in a very relaxed way, as if they're going out on the Sunday club run. But I always do the same thing:

I bounce back on the bike when the starter does the final countdown, 'Five, four . . .'

Then I push back on to the guy holding the back of the bike as if my back wheel is locked into a start gate on the track. I do it even in a one-hour time trial on the road; it's a habit I've maintained from going through that process on the boards so many times.

I hit that first couple of hundred metres as if it was a pursuit: flat out. I always do it. At that point it's so difficult to keep calm. You've been working yourself up into this mental state for the last forty minutes and you're so hyped, so pumped. I have to control myself; I have to say, 'Come on, Bradley, you've still got an hour and five minutes to go here.'

So now I've come down the ramp in Bonneval, made my massive start effort, and then it's time to get a grip. I really back off the pressure, as I always do after that initial big push down the ramp and into the first few hundred metres, and that's where I start to use my power output on the little screen on the handlebars as a guide to keep myself under control. I'm underway so I just settle down into the rhythm of whatever power I've chosen. At Bonneval, the stage started uphill, so naturally you're pushing a lot more power. Get over the top, then settle down. That's where Sean starts talking to me: 'Right, come on, Brad, this is it, this is your area, this is your domain, this is what you do best. Let's settle in.' The power I've chosen is over 450 watts, so on the flat sections I'm looking at holding 450–460 watts, and whenever the road ramps up slightly I'm taking it up to about 470, 480, 490, but again trying not to go over 500 watts, and likewise then, when it was slightly downhill, I'm coming back down to 430.

I can sustain 450 watts for an hour, so obviously the first twenty minutes of that is not difficult. It's a bit like being a 400m runner – running the first 100m should feel relatively easy. In a time trial, the first twenty minutes you're just out there, cruising along. It's about keeping in that controlled state. That's what time trialling is all about, especially over those distances. It's being able to ride that fine line, and keep the concentration, keep the composure. That's the key; that's what makes some people better time triallists than others. So I'm riding along, I'm seeing British cycling fans at the roadside, Union Jacks, posters and things, and every now and again I might think, 'Oh yeah, I'm at 460 watts; that's fine.'

The first reference point in my head is seventeen or eighteen minutes into the stage, because that's when I take a gel. I'm thinking, 'Right, ten minutes gone, ride along a few more minutes; fifteen minutes gone, I've got three minutes until I have to take this gel; so it's eighteen minutes: right, gel, big gel, swig a drink, down, OK, on to phase two.' I use these little markers for myself as well as the time checks out on the course.

By then I've had the first time check, which is at 14km; I'm 12 secs up on Chris Froome: 'Brilliant, perfect, it's all going to plan, that's confirmation of what I'm feeling; I haven't really started pushing on yet and I'm getting twelve seconds already on him . . .' At that point I'm thinking, 'Right, you've got forty-five minutes to go, Brad, you're twelve seconds up, your lead is intact, you're going to win the Tour, let's keep concentrating, you've got forty-five minutes left of everything you've worked for this year; this is it.' I'm really positive, thinking that everything here is confirmation of what I've been doing: 'You deserve this, Brad, this is what you've worked towards . . .'

Sean is talking to me in the earphone all the time, and he's giving me very important information, for example: 'You're coming into a little village now, Brad, there's a slow, sweeping right, it's full.' When he says 'It's full', that means I can stay in the skis – stretched out on the time-trial handlebars. 'No worries, you're coming up now, round this corner there's a sharp left. Back off slightly, take care, you don't need to risk it at this point, hard right, then you're away, then you can get back down to it.' That means I know coming into this village I'm going to be sweeping left, hard right, accelerating out, then I get back on to my rhythm. He's seen the course at least three or four times. He's ridden the course with me in March, he's driven the course the day before, he's driven it in the morning behind one of the other riders, so he's got everything written out in the car next to him. He's constantly giving me that info like a co-driver in a rally.

That time trial's superb for me because it's all long, straight, flat roads – just what I like. A lot of the time you don't remember the whole ride afterwards, just little clips of it. I remember, distinctly, one section after about forty minutes, with about twenty-five minutes left of the race. I'd pushed the pace a little bit above what I was aiming to go at. If I aim for 450 or 460 watts, I'll always push the top part of that, so I was trying to hold 460; and after forty-odd minutes I'd been sustaining this, I knew I was floating;

I was on a good one. We were just going up this small incline, maybe 2 per cent, for a long, long time, and I was motoring up it, and I remember holding 490 odd watts up this rise for a couple of minutes, and then just over the top Sean saying to me, 'You're absolutely flying, Brad, you're eating up the kilometres, I tell you this is impressive.'

The further we go into the race, the more I'm beginning to realize: 'This is it, I've won the Tour, I've done it.' With each kilometre going by, I'm a little more inspired by that thought and that makes me push even more – there is a sort of aggression, a hunger within me, an urge to keep gaining as much time as possible. I want to win this race!

So then we come off the big wide main roads on to smaller roads in the last 10km and it's at that point that it's starting to get painful at this pace. The physical effort is beginning to take its toll: the first twenty minutes are almost easy, the next twenty minutes you're having to concentrate more, but the last twenty minutes is where the pain starts kicking in. But in spite of the pain, I'm still able to lift it up. And at about 5km to go we turn left on to this little road and then the gradient starts ramping up, and I'm still pushing and it's really hurting and with every kilometre that's going past, once we're within 5km to go, I'm beginning to think of a lot of other things – all inspiring me to push on even harder.

5k to go . . .

Sean says, 'You've got 5k to go, Brad, you've got eight minutes left of this Tour de France, eight minutes and you've won the Tour; 4k to go, Brad, six minutes to go and you've won the Tour de France, six minutes left and it's all over.' With those little things that Sean is saying to me I'm thinking, 'This is it, six more minutes,' and my mind starts going back . . .

I'd be going out in December, in the gym at 6 a.m. doing my core work, then getting out on the bike early doors; four hours, five hours; I'd be riding all round Pendle, out on Waddington Fell in a hailstorm, thinking, 'I'm two hours from home now, this is ridiculous, I'm two hours out, how am I going to get home?' I'd get back and my fingers wouldn't bend from the cold, so Cath would have to take the gloves off my hands, but I'd think, 'This is what is going to win the Tour.' It had said four hours on the training programme; it was three degrees outside and it was hailing up there in the hills, but I just had to go and do that four hours because that might make the difference; Cadel Evans might not go out, might not do anything that day . . .

3k to go . . .
Sean is saying, 'Brad, 3k to go, and it's all over, this is it, Brad, this is where all the training's come in, just think of all those rides we were doing in Tenerife . . .'

I'm back in Tenerife and I'm going over those summits in Tenerife, with Shane telling me, 'Come on, Brad, this is where the Tour's won, you know.' It was all for the Tour de France . . .

And here I am with six minutes left of it. This is what it was for . . .

I'm on the phone to Cath when I was in Tenerife training at Easter; the kids were off school, and she was saying 'I wish you were here.' It was Ben's birthday. 'Why are you not here?' he and Bella ask; I tell them and they sort of understand. I say to Cath on the phone,

'Come on, it will be all right, love, this will all be worth it, you know, we're not going to do this for ever . . .' This is what it's been all about; Cath and the kids, all the sacrifices they've made to get me here . . .

We're getting into those last kilometres and I'm thinking of those things, thinking of my childhood, when I started dreaming about the Tour, how I started cycling when I was twelve. I'm about to win the Tour de France, and I'm taking my mind back to riding my bike as a kid going to my grandparents', thinking of everything I've gone through to be at this point now.

There is a lot of pride at what I've achieved and what I've been through to achieve it. And I've led the Tour for two weeks: I look back and think, 'Two weeks. There have been only two leaders of this year's Tour de France.' Bernard Hinault managed two weeks in the jersey once, in 1981; Lance Armstrong never managed it; Eddy Merckx led for longer, but he was the greatest ever.

1k to go . . .
The closer I'm getting to the line, Sean starts

saying to me, 'Come on, Brad, just empty it, 1k to go; 600 metres to go and the Tour's over.' It's always in that way: it's never Sean saying to me, '2k to go, that's it, you've won the Tour'; it's always, 'Come on, Brad, one minute and it's over.'

So I am emptying it to the line as if it is a training effort in Tenerife and I have to get out every last little bit. And that's where the punch in the air happens as I cross the line. It comes from all that emotion I was going through in those last couple of kilometres, for all those hours, all those mornings, all the days before that time trial.

It all comes out in that punch in the air as I go across the line. That's the defining image of the Tour for me: crossing the line and the punch.

It is an incredible, incredible feeling.

AN ENGLISHMAN IN PARIS

There is an iconic image of the final stage of the Tour de France that every cycling fan knows. It shows the peloton lined out along the banks of the Seine when the race is going into the centre of Paris, with the yellow jersey sitting behind his teammates at the front of the bunch, and the Eiffel Tower to the right. I remembered watching this on television as a kid: a team riding down the quays, most often with Miguel Indurain riding behind all his guys in the Banesto blue, red and white. It's an astounding moment for a cycling fan – truly legendary. And on the final Sunday of the 2012 Tour, as we rode along past the Eiffel Tower, there was a brief instant when

I allowed myself to forget I had a job to do that day; suddenly I saw myself riding at the front of the bunch in the same way I had watched Indurain and company while sitting in our little flat in Kilburn all those years ago.

That wasn't the only moment from that Sunday afternoon that will always stay with me. We are on the front, all eight of us from Sky, with Cav sitting behind me at the back of the string as he is going for the sprint. We join the circuit, along the Rue de Rivoli, take a left down through the tunnel and out into the bright sunshine at the exit into the Place de la Concorde. I'm hearing the crowd for the first time, seeing the wall of British flags. It's phenomenal, absolutely phenomenal; as the noise hits us we start riding a decent tempo across the Place de la Concorde towards the Champs-Élysées.

We pedal up the Champs-Élysées, bouncing on the cobbles, past the finish line, past the stands, up to the turn at the top in front of the Arc de Triomphe. I know my family is there in the stands, and as we make the U-turn, the wall of sound from the Brits when I come into sight round the bend is unbelievable.

It was quiet as the first seven riders from Sky took the bend and then, when the Brits see me in the yellow jersey, the noise comes up at me and wallops me in the face.

Amazing.

I'm getting goose pimples. And then of course the attacks start, I'm thrust back to reality, and that's it.

Time to start concentrating – we've got a job to do for Cav.

I'd finished the Tour on the Champs-Élysées three times, and I'd always ridden that stage watching the person who'd won the Tour, imagining the delight he must be feeling. I remember sitting at home in 2011 looking at the television and seeing Cadel doing it, thinking, 'Wow, that must be incredible, knowing the whole race is finished and you've won it.'

It is quite ceremonial, with a whole parade through the suburbs of Paris, and other riders coming up and congratulating you as you ride along. We got all the Sky guys riding abreast across the road for photographs; I posed on the front of the bunch with Peter Sagan, who had won the points jersey, and Thomas Voeckler, who was King of the Mountains. As we were riding in, there were some guys – particularly the French lads – coming up to me and saying, 'Is it all right if I have my photo taken with you?' That felt like the ultimate accolade: the other riders respect you and what you've done so much that they actually want a photo taken to mark the occasion, perhaps so they can show their kids and tell them, '*One day I raced the 2012 Tour and made it to Paris with Bradley Wiggins; he's that bloke in the yellow jersey with the long sideburns.*'

If you are the Tour winner, your team leads the race into Paris, with you sitting behind them. And every minute of that final stage was as sweet as I had expected, as good as it had always looked when I was watching it on television as a kid.

The noise hit me as we turned by the Arc de Triomphe and from that moment on I expected it every lap. You go so fast round the eight laps up and down the Champs-Élysées that you wish it could last for ever, but at the same time you wish it wouldn't because it's quite hard. Relatively speaking, I had a straightforward ride being in yellow, with the other guys giving us a fair bit of road space and letting us get on with it. But even then you know the judges don't stop the clocks until you get to 3km to go – and 6km out there was a serious crash with Danilo Hondo in it. It could, in theory, still be all over at that point.

I'd always wanted to lead Cav out on the Champs-Élysées in the rainbow stripes. I knew the job I had to do: after we came out of the first tunnel I had to take up the running and pull Eddie to about 800 or 700m to go so that he could unleash Cav. It was an exceptional feeling – turning on the power, seeing Cav come past tucked in on Eddie's wheel, then pedalling up the Avenue next to Mick and Richie.

I knew Cav would win. But I had been so focused on what I was doing for him that by the last lap I had forgotten that I had the yellow jersey on. There was no thinking, 'This is the last lap, I've done it, I've won the Tour.' It was, 'It's 3k to go, 2k to go – I'm going to hit the front; 1k – after this tunnel that's it, we're going.' That was the whole thought process for the last couple of laps; then peeling off after I'd done my job for Cav, I was thinking, 'I've done it, I've done what I needed to do for him,' rolling across the Place de la Concorde, turning right up the Champs-Élysées and then I thought, *'I've won the Tour de France!'* It came on me very suddenly because I'd been thinking only about doing that job for Mark.

The finish was a mad rush. Being given the yellow jersey for the last time was strange; I got up on the podium to accept it and shook someone's hand – a young lad. Next thing I know, Bernard Hinault is flying across, and he's chucked this fella off the podium! It's six foot high, and he's just thrown him off the side. I'd shaken this guy's hand, thinking he was the president or somebody, and it turned out he had just got up there; the police grabbed him as he fell.

The second ever Tour de France in 1904 was notorious for skulduggery. Riders were disqualified for catching trains and using cars. When the race passed near to the popular cyclist André Fauré's hometown, fans tried to jump in front of other riders passing through. The trouble was only solved after race officials fired shots in the air. These events led to the disqualification of every stage winner, as well as the top four finishers, though the exact reasons were never officially made public.

I was conscious of all the British fans being there, so on the podium I made a point of turning towards them. You can look up the Champs-Élysées and see a sea of Union Jacks waving right up to the Arc de Triomphe so that is where all the fans were.

It was bizarre, and part of me was still thinking, 'I'm not supposed to win the Tour de France.' I never, ever considered myself in the same bracket as people like Hinault and Merckx, people like Miguel Indurain who I'd watched winning the Tour. Now I was standing up there as the winner!

If I ever look at the video of me on the podium, the way I behave on the podium pretty much sums up how stunned I was. When Lesley Garrett sang 'God Save the Queen' it felt a bit embarrassing being up there – that's why I made a little crack about picking the raffle prizes, like I've done at dozens of British cycling club dinners over the years. As a fan of the sport, part of me will always feel I'm just Brad, not in the same class as Hinault or Indurain. I believe in myself as an athlete, but the bit of me that's a fan of the sport will never accept I'm comparable with them.

I rode down the Champs with my son Ben on his little yellow Pinarello, and my daughter Isabella behind in the car. That was surreal again; I remember taking the yellow jersey off after the podium, and that's when I jumped on the team car in my Sky kit. Everyone was looking at me, and I couldn't think what to do, so I just jumped on top of the car.

I didn't want to wear the yellow jersey on the

TEAM SKY

NAME	COUNTRY	YEAR OF BIRTH	HEIGHT	WEIGHT	SPECIALISM	TOUR DE FRANCE WINS
Edvald Boasson Hagen	Norway	1987	1.81m	73kg	Time trial/ Sprinter/ All rounder	2 stages (2011)
Mark Cavendish	Great Britain	1985	1.75m	69kg	Sprinter	Points Classification (2011), 23 stages (2008–2012)
Bernhard Eisel	Austria	1981	1.83m	78kg	Classics Specialist	
Chris Frome	Great Britain	1985	1.86m	69kg	All rounder	1 stage (2012)
Christian Knees	Germany	1981	1.94m	81kg	Rouleur	
Richie Porte	Australia	1985	1.72m	62kg	Time trial	
Michael Rogers	Australia	1979	1.85m	75kg	All rounder	
Kanstantsin Siutsou	Belarus	1982	1.84m	68kg	All rounder	
Bradley Wiggins	Great Britain	1980	1.90m	69kg	Time trial/ All rounder	General Classification (2012); 2 stages (2012)

lap of honour: I didn't want to be singled out as the yellow jersey – I wanted to be with the team. I didn't really like it when they picked me up on their shoulders. We'd done it together, I couldn't have done it without them, and I didn't want it to be just about me.

Then we were all whisked off to the Ritz to have a little reception, after which it was a mad rush. We had to sprint off and get our bags together; then we were home six hours later.

It was all done.

When Cath and I walked in through the front door of the house, it was the point when we had to start dealing with the fact that I'd just won the Tour. I also had to get myself organized – there were only five days before the Olympic road race!

I'd won the Tour de France, but I felt as if I would be the last person to take it on board; it reminded me a little of how I felt when I won the Olympic pursuit for the first time in 2004. It's almost a kind of disbelief that this is happening; it's little things like seeing my picture in the yellow jersey on the front page of a magazine. You don't realize it's you on there. It's strange. And there are messages like the one I had from Sir Chris Hoy, who said he thought the Tour win was the greatest achievement ever in British sport: it's humbling to hear praise of that kind. The biggest accolade is respect from your peers, people I look up to.

The build-up all through 2012 had not been just about the Tour de France though. We had also been thinking about the Olympic road race and in particular the time trial there. All the training from 1 November 2011 had been about backing up, being able to work hard day after day, back to back, being fit enough to sustain the workload to win the Tour. With that under my belt, if I stayed healthy, the one-hour Olympic time trial nine days after the Tour was going to be a doddle in comparison. There was definitely no question of simply seeing what happened when we got to the end of the Tour. The plans for 22 July and afterwards were put in place well before the Dauphiné.

I'd insisted on going home first. It was what I'd looked forward to throughout the Tour, but being back in Lancashire wasn't quite what I expected. The very next day people started knocking on the door. That Monday morning, there were cars parked for half a mile down the road. We woke up to find a mass of press and other people outside, so it felt as if we were under siege. All of a sudden a lot had changed. I'd under-estimated quite how big the whole thing would be. By the evening I was saying, 'I've got to go out on my bike for an hour,' so I went for a quick spin, but at first I couldn't get through the mass of people, and I had to give the journalists a few minutes.

There was a line of cars following me as I rode, people taking photographs, people wanting me to sign things – and the next day when I went out to the Co-op for a pint of milk and a loaf of bread I was mobbed. The same thing happened when I took Ben to a rugby-league training day; all the rugby people kept coming over, which you don't expect because cycling isn't their thing. We met Sam Tomkins, a Wigan hero, and there he was praising me.

Cycling is a sport that levels people out. When you go on a club run, if you puncture you repair it yourself. You don't get someone else to do it for you. I still wash my own bike when I'm at home and it gets covered in muck – I did that the Monday after the Tour. I was laughed at and called names when I was a kid wearing Lycra — not the thing to do in the 1990s. As cyclists we become famous in our own little world, but we don't usually become celebrities.

It all takes a bit of getting used to.

LONDON CALLING

On the Thursday after the Tour finished, I was down in Surrey at the Great Britain team hotel.

The GB squad is an environment that I love. Being with them feels like coming home. I'd been a member of the British Cycling team since July 1998, when Peter Keen called me into his office in the Manchester velodrome and signed me up to what was initially known as the World Class Performance Programme. Back then, his vision was for Britain to be the number one cycling nation, but it was all about the Olympics, rather than the Tour, like in professional road cycling. Credit for the British

Cycling team's recent success is rightly given to Dave Brailsford, and it's an amusing thought that he joined World Class at the same time as me. Since I was eighteen and walked into the Manchester velodrome and saw Dave for the first time, he's been a bit like a mischievous older brother to me. If Cav is like my younger brother, Dave is the one who is a lot older, not just a couple of years older, but maybe a ten- or fifteen-year age gap.

Dave was in charge when I won on the track in Athens and Beijing; and he's always been incredibly supportive. There are two things with Dave. One is that he has always given me whatever I've needed to succeed, be it bikes, coaching, racing. The other thing with Dave is that I've never had a telling-off face to face from him. I think what happens is that he gets het up about me when I'm not there, but when he sees me walk into his office he sees me as a person and he understands me.

If you look for the secret of his success, I think you have to remember that Dave is not a coach, and although he's raced a bike, it wasn't at a high level. He's a hard worker, a grafter. He'll sit in that velodrome for five, six, seven days for weeks on end and runs British Cycling from top to bottom. He knows every in and out of it: who, where and what. He's not just some kind of chief executive figure who you never see.

It's hard for me to put my finger on what has made British Cycling so successful, because it's been part of my life for so long now. One of the major things that British Cycling, or World Class as it was, has always had is a central base – the velodrome in Manchester. Gradually, over the years, all the team riders and staff started moving into the area so the velodrome became the daily training venue, whether you were meeting to go out on the road, putting the hours in on the track, going in to see a physio, or working out in the gyms. I think that makes a huge difference. It's a bit like a football team training at the same facility every day.

Olympic fever!

During the week before the Olympics, Dave rang me and said, 'Look, they want you to ring the bell at the Olympic opening ceremony. It's massive – you know you can't say no to it.' It was important that doing it wouldn't disrupt our preparation for the road race, which was the morning after, so I said to Dave, 'So long as you are happy for me to do it, you organize it and I'll do it.'

That whole period was very surreal. We had a taste of how big it all was when we went out training as a team before the Olympic road race, and people who were just going about their daily business were saying, 'Hey, there go Great Britain!' The support was massive in the villages around the team hotel, and on Box Hill there were people everywhere looking for a glimpse of us and all the others. You could feel the buzz.

We drove across to the Olympic village, which was incredible – I love that atmosphere, the feeling you get from being in the village with all the other athletes. I wasn't going to get it at this Games, as we were staying in Surrey, so this was my only chance to experience it. I'd arranged to meet Chris Hoy in there, and we had a meal in the Olympic village together, with all kinds of people looking at us. Chris was carrying the flag that night for Great Britain in the opening ceremony parade, and after he went off to join the team, Dave and I walked over to the stadium. It was a matter of taking everything in my stride; 'Oh yeah, we're going to go to the opening ceremony . . .'

I stand backstage, wearing the yellow jersey that they gave me, wired up in the way that bands are on arena tours, so they can hear the backing tracks. It feels rather like wearing earplugs. Someone says, 'OK, Bradley, on in two seconds.'

They open the door: 'Go.'

I walk to the front of the stage, stop at the cross marked on the floor; wave to the crowd. All I can see is a wall of flashing lights. I can't hear anything except the sound of my breathing in my ears . . .

'All right, Bradley, turn round, go up to the bell, stand at the bell and wait for your command to ring it.'

I ring the bell, walk down the steps and out of the stadium . . .

Someone threw a jacket over me and I was whisked straight out. I was on the stage at the opening ceremony at two minutes past nine, and by half past I was back in the hotel with the

Great Britain boys. In no time I was changed into team kit to talk through the next day and work out how we were going to do everything we could to win the Olympic road race for Cav. Then I had to go and shave my legs, pin my numbers on and go through all the pre-race routine for the next morning.

The whole country was expecting us to produce a gold medal in the first event of the Games. The minute that was done, my thoughts had to turn to my time trial event. Maybe in twenty years' time I'll look back and tell my grandchildren, 'Oh yeah, the Olympic Games in London, I was there, I did the thing with the bell.' It was fantastic to be asked. It was definitely special to play a part in some way.

But I had no idea what public opinion was about what I'd done at the Tour. I hadn't been anywhere in public other than the Co-op in the village to get a pint of milk. I'd been in a bubble.

That might explain what happened when I was waiting to go out into the stadium to ring the bell. When we got there, the volunteer at the entrance said, 'It's quite good in that stadium, you know.'

So I asked, 'I'm not going to get booed or something, am I?'

'Trust me,' he said. 'No, you won't get booed.'

THE ROLLERCOASTER

Sitting in the minibus as we were driven to the start of the Olympic road race on The Mall, I could see Mark Cavendish's leg twitching. Cav is quite a fidgety guy; he's always bouncing around — I think it's a sprinter's thing. When he's sitting down, he's always twitching his legs, rocking his leg on the heel of his foot as if he's pumping up a camp bed with a footpump. He does it constantly: when we are on the bus in the morning, when he's eating; this time, I had a feeling I knew what was in his mind.

I said, 'You'll be all right, mate, you'll be fine. We'll take this thing on.'

In the days before, as we had pottered through

the Surrey lanes on little training rides, Cav had seemed like a man with the weight of the nation on his shoulders. He was paying particular attention to every little detail: looking at his bike, making sure his overshoes were right, checking that his shoes were exactly what he wanted. It's not often that you see a rider as pumped for a single event as he was.

DID YOU KNOW?

The first ever bicycle race took place in 1868, in the Parc de Saint-Cloud, Paris. An Englishman called James Moore won the 1,200m race with a wooden bicycle with iron tyres.

During the Tour, Cav had been extremely understanding about the situation we were in; that is why I wanted to ride for him at the Olympics until I had nothing left in my legs. All year, until we got to July, I had been thinking, 'Ah, the Olympic road race – I'm just going to do what I have to do and get out.' I so desperately wanted Mark to win at the Olympics and he was only doing this one event. The very least I owed him was to give it everything.

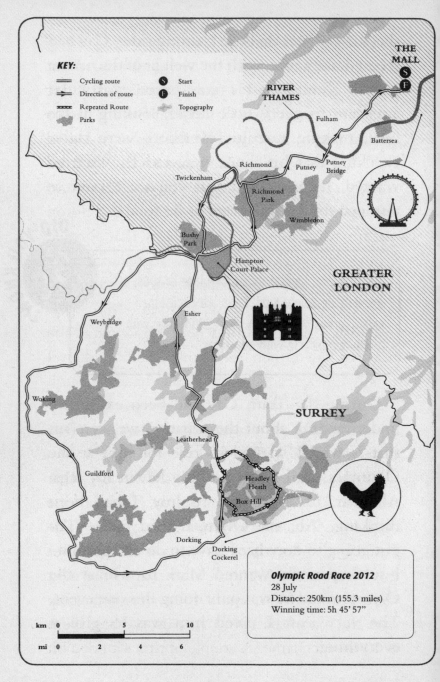

KEY:

Cycling route
Direction of route
Repeated Route
Parks

S Start
F Finish
Topography

THE MALL

RIVER THAMES

Fulham

Battersea

Richmond

Putney

Putney Bridge

Twickenham

Richmond Park

Wimbledon

Bushy Park

Hampton Court Palace

GREATER LONDON

Weybridge

Esher

Woking

SURREY

Leatherhead

Guildford

Headley Heath

Box Hill

Dorking

Dorking Cockerel

Olympic Road Race 2012
28 July
Distance: 250km (155.3 miles)
Winning time: 5h 45' 57"

km 0   5   10
mi 0   2   4   6

Road racing at London 2012

The course started in The Mall and headed out through south-west London into Surrey for nine laps around Box Hill. Great Britain had to get on the case early. The four of us – David Millar, Froomie, Ian Stannard and I – started riding at the front of the peloton just 20km into the race. The plan was to keep the peloton within reach of any lead groups that formed around the Box Hill circuits, so that the race would regroup coming back into London and then Cav could put his sprint to good use.

It was a long day: I'd been working at the head of the bunch for about 220km when I finally peeled off as we came back through Knightsbridge, with 4 or 5km to go. I think I spent six of the nine laps on the front up Box Hill.

We had experimented with the intensity that we needed to be riding at on the climb on one of the days when we were training there. The first lap, I went up it at 440 watts; the other guys were attacking up it after that so the next time I was at 450; again they were attacking over the top of that, but I was just holding them at 100m each time. A couple of times it got a bit lively up there so I was pushing it up to 460, and by the last time up the hill, a little peloton of 33 had come together at the front.

But then it just didn't work out over those final miles. It needed another team or two to come to the front and work, but none of them wanted to help Cav get to the finish. Ironically, if a team with a sprinter had put some graft in, they'd have beaten him on The Mall, as he finished with a slow puncture and wasn't able to sprint properly.

As the gold medal was presented to Alexander Vinokourov of Kazakhstan – a rider who had tested positive for doping in 2007 – we sat in the tent in the pits for an hour after the finish with our skinsuits unzipped. We were too exhausted to get changed, and just too depressed. It was as if we'd all lost the race – all five of us – or as if we'd lost a man during war. I was gutted we hadn't won, and it felt as if some of our rivals were really pleased to see us fail, so that left us all a bit upset.

I think the press really did build Cav up a bit too much though – and I don't think he'd fully appreciated how hard it is to win an Olympic road race with a small team. All the headlines that night were along the lines of, 'Cav fails to win Britain's first gold medal of the Olympic Games.' I even saw one story that read, 'Even Bradley Wiggins was struggling to hold the pace at the end,' asking if our 'failure' might be due to fatigue from the Tour de France. You read that and you think, 'Are you serious, did you not see me riding on the front for over two hundred kilometres?'

The last two weeks of the Tour had looked pretty straightforward. There had been no massive dramas or nail-biting suspense once I got the yellow jersey – so having watched that for fourteen days, most of the press just assumed that when it came to the Olympic road race Great Britain would carry on where Sky left off. The problem was that a one-day race on a hilly course with a five-man team is a completely different matter to a three-week Tour with nine men.

After the race, I was going back to the team hotel and Cav was heading straight off to race in Belgium and France; he hugged me, and I said, 'I'll see you later.' Then he sent me a text before the time trial saying, 'Go and bash them all tomorrow.'

That night I was totally on my knees, and the day after I was still absolutely shattered. But we had a good team routine at Foxhills – recovering, sleeping, out on the bikes – and by the third day I started feeling really good again. The chances were, I needed that ride in the road race to open me up, having stopped after the Tour for a few days.

During the Tour it had struck us that on each of the occasions when I had won a time trial all year Sean Yates had been there, so I asked him if he wanted to be driving the car behind me in London. He said, 'I'd love to do it, will I get a tracksuit?' so he came along, drove the course the day before, and rode it; that meant he had all that information and he and I could talk together during the trial in the same way we had in every time trial I'd ridden all season.

It was the same process I had been through at the Tour and every other time trial in recent years. So that put me in Hampton Court on the Wednesday morning, feeling super-confident that I could win. All I had to do was go out and put my ride together.

All year we had been looking to move closer

to Fabian Cancellara – one of my biggest rivals for Olympic gold – in every way. It was similar to the approach Great Britain had adopted on the track – you analyse where you are, see where the rest of the world is, and you look at what they're doing.

It was the same with time trialling, and the big thing we had flagged up with Fabian was how much time he took out of the other riders just because he was better at cornering. That was always one area we were looking to improve in.

With Tony Martin – the other big challenger for gold – it was more about looking at his cadence. I tended to spin a lower gear, partly because of my background as a track cyclist, where fast pedalling is a key element. He was turning the pedals a good 15 or 20rpm slower than me. So we worked on torque all through the winter of 2011–12, simply putting more power into my pedalling but at lower revs. We started with five-minute blocks and progressed through the winter – seven-and-a-half-minute blocks, fifteen-minute blocks – until before the Tour I was doing forty-minute climbs at threshold at 50rpm. We had known it would take me a long time to build up to that kind of time and torque – that was why we had had to start in November.

Now, in Hampton Court in August 2012, I was very relaxed. I remember talking to my mechanic Diego beforehand, and him saying, 'Brad I've got something to tell you.'

'What is it, Diego?'

'On the way to the start we went round this roundabout and your bike wasn't attached properly to the roof and it fell off and it smashed your handlebars.'

'What – my race bike . . . ?'

'No, your spare bike.'

He had to put some other handlebars on the second bike, which weren't the same as the ones on the race bike, but I just sat there laughing. 'Don't worry about that, Diego, I'm not going to need a spare bike today!'

That sums up the state of mind I was in at the time. In the Tour, and in the first few days after the Tour, I remember thinking that if I could just get a medal of any colour in London that would be fantastic. Now I was raring to go. I was just thinking about the process: the walk up the ramp, launching myself out of the start house, not getting carried away too early on, and all the steps through the ride, fuelling after seventeen minutes and so on.

The minute I turned up in the start area, I couldn't believe the roar I got. I remember sitting in the stage area next to the ramp and getting a buzz from the crowd. Then I rolled down the ramp and the sound of the crowd really hit me.

I turned left out of the ticketed area, onto Hampton Court Bridge, and the noise was unbelievable. It was the same all the way around that course, but the bit I will always remember to the day I die was going through the last time check. It was at 9km to go, just before Kingston, and Sean told me I was 29secs ahead of Tony Martin: knowing that there were only about five miles to go, all I had to do was keep it together and I was going to win!

I remember going through Kingston, not taking any super risks on the couple of little corners, through a shopping precinct; then over Kingston Bridge and down to a roundabout. I had to slow down quite a bit, coming out of the roundabout, and because I'd pulled up, I was then accelerating away almost from a standing start. The road had narrowed down so the yells and screams from the crowd were actually deafening, to the point where I got ringing in my ears.

Then it was a matter of giving it everything I had all the way to the finish.

I turned into Bushy Park towards the end, and I could see Tony Martin's cars up the road, so I knew I'd beaten him. At that point you're emptying it, you're nailed, you're just trying to keep it together; I kept giving more than I had to, thinking, 'Empty it to the line'; I'd lift the pace quite a bit and then I'd bring it back down, because I knew I couldn't sustain it. I was already fifty minutes into the ride and thinking, 'No, no, you don't need to do that, Brad, just hold it, hold it, you don't need to push like that.' I was continually doing that in those last few kilometres, even when it was clear I'd got it in the bag.

Coming round that last sweeping bend and up to the line, the crowd seemed to go dead silent. I was thinking, 'Uh oh.' Normally everyone cheers when you cross the line so I thought, 'I've lost it! I must have done something to have lost it!' Then the crowd erupted and that had to be for me, but I still wasn't certain.

I kept saying, 'Have I got the fastest time?'

'Yeah, you got the fastest time.'

'Are you sure?'

'Yeah, yeah.'

The exhaustion began hitting me; I had to sit down for a bit.

'Is Fabian in yet? Is Fabian in yet?'

'No, no.' But eventually Fabian came in and they said, 'That's it – you've done it!'

So I stood up again, went up into the finish area where people were cheering and I was trying to soak it all in. They directed me to the throne which they had been putting each of the leaders on as they waited for their time to be beaten; I sat there for a second and did a Winston Churchill victory sign – it's that picture that everyone printed.

And then it was time to get the medal . . . Olympic gold!

Sometime later, when they were selling off the bits and pieces after the Games, I asked if I could have that throne as a memento. They wanted £100,000 for it because there was so much interest in it, so I told them they should find another customer!

WHAT NEXT?

That time trial has to rate as my greatest Olympic moment. To win that gold medal in that setting, in London, in front of Hampton Court, with all the history going back to Henry VIII – it was about as British as you can get.

Every athlete has a defining year during their career. Sir Chris Hoy's was Beijing when he won his three gold medals, and 2012 is probably mine. For the best part of an hour that Wednesday in Surrey, I was able to savour that feeling, of being at my best, with a massive crowd deafening me with their support. It was astounding; I am never going to experience anything like that again in my sporting life. Nothing is ever going to top that.

Ever since, I've been trying to take it all in, wondering whether that time trial was my greatest sporting moment. Was it better than the Tour de France? In my eyes, the Tour will always be phenomenal because of what the team did for me. I did the job, but the whole race – all twenty-two days of it – was about the team putting me in a position to win. I will never forget it.

Part of what drives me is the love and respect I feel for the sport and its history. That goes back to my childhood. I grew up with posters of the great cyclists on my bedroom walls, while other kids were into football. A childhood dream was to go and lift the FA Cup because that was what those great players had achieved, but for me as a kid, the dream was to lead a race like the Dauphiné, or even the Tour for one day.

There haven't been many Tour winners in my lifetime, perhaps a dozen, so it's a very special list to be on. You never imagine you will be up there with the top names – Millar, Simpson, Hinault, Merckx and so on. You never imagine that not only will you be the winner of the Tour, but you'll also win Paris–

Nice, Dauphiné and the Tour of Romandie in the same year, which is incredible.

I've always loved cycling because it's you against the machine. You apply yourself to something in your life, and then it's all about numbers, judgement, putting the ride together, having it all go to plan. You do the training, you get this power – it's that simple, and I love the sense of accomplishment. It's nice to be recognized and get respect for being good at something, and it's incredible that sport can do that, although it is just sport and you can't lose sight of that.

I think the difference between the Olympic gold medal and the Tour is that the time trial was all about me. It was all about my individual performance on the day – about what I could put together nine days after the Tour. As an individual feat it was probably the best sporting performance of my career and it will stick in my mind as my greatest ride, the peak of my physical condition.

The margin of victory was significant, and to do it on those roads and in that atmosphere was incredible. It had been raining in the morning and it seemed as if the sun came out just for those few hours; it was a great, great occasion. People simply didn't want to go home afterwards – as if they wanted the day to go on for ever.

Looking back to 2010, it was as if everything I did seemed to go wrong, no matter how I tried; in 2012 it was as if I could do no wrong. I've kind of got a bit of everything in there as all the wins in 2012 were different – a time trial, winning that bunch kick in the Tour of Romandie, climbing to win the Dauphiné, and then the defining images of the Tour, all followed up by an Olympic time-trial gold medal. But it's been as if *everything* I did seemed to turn to gold.

I don't know what the future holds. The London Games was always going to be a massive goal – I never looked further ahead than 1 August 2012 and that time trial.

I struggle with the idea that I may have turned into a role model overnight. People say to me, 'Are you ready now, do you realize you are a role model for so many people out there?' I can understand why – for what I do on the bike – but please don't hold me up there as something to aspire to, because outside a sports environment I'm as normal as everyone else. I'm not perfect. I make mistakes. I've got a normal life like everyone else. I have a different job to everyone else, but I have a family, and it's not easier because of what you do or what you get paid.

Adapting to what 2012 has brought me may not be easy. Trying to be as good as I could be in the Tour, and if possible winning it, was something that Cath, Ben, Isabella and I bought into together. It was a complete lifestyle, twelve months of the year – and that's what we have lived by for four years. It was worth the sacrifice in 2012 to do it all once, but it's hard to say if it would be worth it to do it all again. And if I do it again, do I go out and try and win a third?

In many ways, I don't want to go back to the Tour ever again. If I were to go back and my heart was not in it, or I hadn't done the work, I'd be in big trouble. If I can't do it 110 per cent to win, I'd rather not be there.

I also have other goals. I have said I'd like to do another two years at this level, so that means I only have two years in which to win other events I feel are important – such as the Giro d'Italia and Paris–Roubaix. After that I would like to go back on the track squad for two years, go for gold in the Olympic team pursuit in Rio in 2016. Returning to the track would be a different challenge, but I like the idea of a different type of commitment: to be a pure track rider, a pure endurance rider.

So that's my plan: to go through to 2014, riding the Commonwealth Games, then becoming a track rider again, still racing on the road, but the road would only be to build my fitness for the track.

Glasgow 2014, Commonwealth Games.
World Championships 2015.
Olympics 2016.
And that would be that!

I've sometimes wondered what my granddad George would have thought of all that has happened to me and the family in the two years since we lost him. As my father figure and the man who helped me develop a love of all sports, he'd have been made up to see me succeed for sure, but there's one other thing.

During the Games, there was speculation about whether I might end up with a knighthood in the same way that Sir Chris Hoy did after his great year. People asked me about it, so I did wonder whether I'd accept it if it were to come my way. I can never see myself being given a title like Sir Bradley Wiggins – it's not what happens to kids from Kilburn! And I've never considered myself above anybody else.

I said to my nan, 'If I get offered a knighthood or whatever, what do you reckon George would make of it if I turned it down?'

She came back, quick as a flash: 'He would never have spoken to you again.'

Sir Bradley Wiggins CBE was knighted in the 2013 New Year's Honours for services to cycling, just days after winning the 2012 BBC Sports Personality of the Year Award.

ACKNOWLEDGEMENTS

Without these people none of this would have happened. I am indebted to:

Everyone at Team Sky, but particular thanks to Dave Brailsford, Shane Sutton, Tim Kerrison, Sean Yates, Rod Ellingworth, Dan the physio, Diego, Mario, Gary, Alldis and all the other backroom staff.

The Tour boys: Mick Rogers, Richie Porte, Christian Knees, Chris Froome, Mark Cavendish, Bernhard Eisel, Kosta Siutsou, Edvald Boasson Hagen.

Faces from the peloton: Steve Cummings, Matt Rabin. Team GB: Matt Parker, Nigel Mitchell, Doug Dailey, Luc de Wilde, Phil Burt, Richard Freeman, Alan Williams, the lads in the stores, all the boys in the workshop.

For help with the book I'd like to thank William Fotheringham, and everybody at Yellow Jersey Press, including Matt Phillips,

Frances Jessop, James Jones, Bethan Jones, Phil Brown, Penny Liechti, Monique Corless, Justine Taylor, Alice Brett, Myra Jones, Ben Murphy, Richard Cable, Roger Bratchell and Tom Drake-Lee. My agent Jonathan Marks and his partner-in-crime Emma Wade, and everyone else at MTC.

All the lads at Paul Hewitt Cycles for building wheels for me, Terry Dolan and Steve, Richard and Mick from Sport and Publicity, Mark at Adidas, Scott Mitchell.

I'd like to thank those a little closer to home too. My mum, my nan, George – who would have loved to see everything that's happened this last twelve months – and everyone else who makes up Team Wiggins. My parents-in-law Liz and Dave, Ruth and Neil.

Finally Cath, Ben and Bella. Thank you for giving me the gift of patience and under-standing to allow me to follow my dream. And thanks for always reminding me what's most important.

APPENDIX I

A CYCLING GLOSSARY

breakaway: when a rider, or group of riders, manages to get ahead of the main *peloton* with a sudden burst

bunch sprint: occasions where riders arrive near the finish line in large numbers and fight to arrange their sprinters in the best positions to reach top speeds. This is often a very fast moment of the race

cadence: the rate at which a cyclist pedals (in revolutions per minute)

Classic: classic cycle races are one-day professional cycling road races

climber: a rider who takes the strain when the team go up steep slopes and mountains

col: the lowest point of a mountain ridge connecting two peaks *contre-la-montre:* time trial event

directeur sportif: the person who plans the tactics for a team road race, then makes sure the riders are fully informed and supported during the race itself

domestiques: members of a road cycling team who are charged with keeping the key members – the leader and any sprint specialist, for instance – protected, keeping them safe from crashes and carrying the food and water for the whole team

doping: using drugs to enhance performance. Cheating, basically

Giro d'Italia, the: a multiple-stage major road cycling event held annually in Italy

hammer: 'putting the hammer down' means really pedalling hard

keirin: a 2,000m track event in which riders follow a pace-setter on a moped round the track for a specified number of laps, then sprint to the finishing line

kinesio tape: an adhesive elastic cotton strip used to support joints and muscles

lactic acid: a naturally produced substance that builds in a person's muscles after anaerobic exercise (like pedalling); this is what makes your muscles stiff the day after exercise if you overdo it!

Madison: a track cycling event in which teams of two (or three) riders ride alternately, with rest periods in between rides

maillot jaune: the yellow jersey in the Tour de France

patron: the unofficial leader of the peloton riding group, often the most respected, who decides when to break for nature calls and when to ride in single file

peloton: also called the field, bunch or pack, this is the main group in a road race

prologue: a short time trial before the first stage of a race over several days; it decides who wears the yellow jersey on the first day

road cycling: cycling events held over roads, climbing up mountains and going through villages and towns; the events can be anything from one-day time trials, to three-day events, to three-weekers like the Tour de France

skis: time-trial handlebars that are long, so that riders can rest their arms along them to achieve a lower position that is more aerodynamic

slipstreaming: riding close behind other riders to help save energy; the reduction in drag is significant and can be as much as 40% in the middle of an organized team. Also known as drafting

soigneur: a Pro team assistant who looks after the riders when they arrive at events; they are responsible for feeding, clothing, and escorting riders

sportif: organized long-distance, mass-participation cycling events that are not considered to be races

sprinters: riders who specialize in short, sharp bursts of speed to sprint the final stages of a race

SRMs: the cranks that measure a cyclist's power output, pulse rate, speed, etc.

stage racing: a race held over the course of several days or weeks in which competitors ride across long distance

team pursuit: a track cycling event involving (usually) four riders

tempo: the steady rate at which a rider at the front of a group is cycling, often measured in revs per minute (revolutions – or turns of the wheel – each minute)

threshold: the point at which you can work

where your body can just about cope with the demands you put on it (lactic acid is being produced and processed at the same rate)

time trial: a race where riders go off at time intervals and each rider's time over the course is recorded with the winner being the fastest; time triallists need to be able to keep up a high, steady speed over a long distance

torque: a measure of the turning force on an object, e.g. a foot on a pedal

Tour de France: a major road cycling event held annually over three weeks in France every July

Tour of Britain: a multi-stage cycling race that takes place every September in Great Britain

track cycling: cycling events held on special tracks; they include both sprints and endurance events

TSS: *Training Stress Score* – scores produced by computer software that show how hard a rider has been working

turbo trainer: a tripod with a weighted roller on it. Riders slot the back wheel of the bike into the tripod, settle the back tyre on to the roller, then ramp up the resistance to the required level and pedal away. Used both for training and for warming up just before a race begins

UCI World Tour: a league of professional racing teams which ranks riders and keeps all the records over the season

VAM: *velocità ascensionale media* – average climbing speed, or how quickly you gain height in a climb

velodrome: an arena built specially for cycling races, which usually features banked oval tracks

Vuelta a España: a major multiple-stage road cycling event held annually in Spain

watts: a unit of power, which is the rate at which energy is produced or used

yellow jersey: worn by the overall leader of the race at the end of each stage

APPENDIX II:

THE GOLDEN YEAR

My major successes in the 2012 season

FEBRUARY 15–19: VOLTA AO ALGARVE, PORTUGAL

Stage five: Lagoa – Portimão, 25.8km individual time trial
Winner: Bradley Wiggins (GB) Team Sky in 0-32-48
Overall:
Winner: Richie Porte (Australia) Team Sky 19-02-43
3rd: Bradley Wiggins at 44sec

MARCH 4–11: PARIS–NICE, FRANCE

Stage one: Dampierre-en-Yvelines – Saint-Rémy-les-Chevreuse, 9.4km individual time trial
Winner: Gustav Larsson (Sweden) Vacansoleil-DCM in 0-11-19
2nd: Bradley Wiggins at 1sec

Stage five: Onet-le-Château – Mende, 178.5km
Winner: Lieuwe Westra (Netherlands)
Vacansoleil-DCM in 4-52-46
3rd: Bradley Wiggins at 6sec
Stage eight: Nice – Col d'Èze 9.6km individual
time trial
Winner: Bradley Wiggins (GB) Team Sky in
0-19-12
Overall:
Winner: Bradley Wiggins (GB) Team Sky in
28-12-16

APRIL 24–29: TOUR OF ROMANDIE, SWITZERLAND

Stage one: Morges – La Chaux-de-Fonds, 184.5km
Winner: Bradley Wiggins (GB) Team Sky in
4-50-23
Stage five: Crans-Montana – Crans-Montana,
16.5km individual time trial
Winner: Bradley Wiggins (GB) Team Sky in
0-28-56
Overall:
Winner: Bradley Wiggins (GB) Team Sky in
18-05-40

JUNE 3–10: CRITÉRIUM DU DAUPHINÉ, FRANCE

Prologue: Grenoble – Grenoble, 5.7km individual
time trial

Winner: Luke Durbridge (Australia) Orica
GreenEDGE in 0-06-38
2nd: Bradley Wiggins at 1sec
Stage four: Villié-Morgon – Bourg-en-Bresse,
53.5km individual time trial
Winner: Bradley Wiggins (GB) Team Sky in
1-03-12
Stage six: Saint-Alban-Leysse – Morzine, 167.5km
Winner: Nairo Quintana (Columbia) Movistar in
4-46-12
4th: Bradley Wiggins at 24sec
Overall:
Winner: Bradley Wiggins (GB) Team Sky in
26-40-46

JUNE 30–JULY 22: TOUR DE FRANCE, FRANCE

Prologue: Liège – Liège, 6.4km individual time
trial
Winner: Fabian Cancellara (Switzerland)
RadioShack-Nissan in 0-07-13
2nd: Bradley Wiggins at 7sec
Stage seven: Tomblaine – La Planche des Belles
Filles, 199km
Winner: Chris Froome (GB) Team Sky in
4-58-35
3rd: Bradley Wiggins at 2sec
Stage eight: Belfort – Porrentruy, 157.5km
Winner: Thibaut Pinot (France) Francais Des

Jeux–BigMat in 3-56-10

4th: Bradley Wiggins at 26sec

Stage nine: Arc-et-Senans – Besançon 41.5km
individual time trial

Winner: Bradley Wiggins (GB) Team Sky in
0-51-24

Stage seventeen: Bagnères-de-Luchon – Peyragudes,
143.5km

Winner: Alejandro Valverde (Spain) Movistar in
4-12-11

3rd: Bradley Wiggins at 19sec

Stage nineteen: Bonneval – Chartres, 53.5km
individual time trial

Winner: Bradley Wiggins (GB) Team Sky in
1-04-13

Overall:

Winner: Bradley Wiggins (GB) Team Sky in
87-34-47sec

2nd: Chris Froome (GB) Team Sky at 3min 21sec

3rd: Vincenzo Nibali (Italy) Liquigas-
Cannondale at 6min 19sec

AUGUST 1: OLYMPIC GAMES, LONDON

Individual time trial, 44km

Gold: Bradley Wiggins (GB) in 0-50-39

LIST OF ILLUSTRATIONS

1. Bradley Wiggins with his father, Gary Wiggins; childhood photographs (all courtesy of Maureen Cousins)

2. Racing as a junior (all courtesy of Maureen Cousins)

3. After winning gold in the individual pursuit at the Beijing Olympic Games in 2008 (Cameron Spencer/Getty); a lap of honour with Paul Manning, Chris Newton and Bryan Steel after winning bronze in the team pursuit at the Sydney Olympic Games in 2000 (Pool JO/Gamma-Rapho/Getty Images); the Madison with Rob Hayles at the Athens Olympic Games in 2004 (Greg Wood/AFP/Getty); riding in the 2010 Tour de France (Bryn Lennon/Getty)

4–5. The peloton at the start of the 2011 Tour de France (Joel Saget/Getty)

6. Mark Cavendish after winning the road race at the 2011 Road World Championships in Copenhagen (Press Association); leading out at the road race (Graham Watson)

7. Waiting at the start in the peloton (Scott Mitchell)

8. Greeting fans arriving at the stage start (Scott Mitchell); Bradley Wiggins (Scott Mitchell)

9. With the press (Scott Mitchell)

10. A training ride in Majorca in 2012 (Bryn Lennon/Getty); encouragement from fans during the 2012 Tour de France (Tim De Waele/Corbis); in yellow at Paris–Nice in 2012 (Bryn Lennon/Getty)

11. Punching the air after winning the final time trial (Bryn Lennon/Getty)

12. Riding into Paris with Sky teammates during the final stage; in the team bus (both Scott Mitchell)

13. With wife, Cath, in Paris (Tim De Waele/Corbis); celebrating winning the Tour (Scott Mitchell)

14. The road race at the 2012 London Olympic Games (Visionhaus/Corbis); ready to race in the individual time trial (Carl de Souza/Getty)

15. Racing in the individual time trial (Tim De Waele/Corbis)

16. On the podium during the victory ceremony at Hampton Court Palace (Alex Livesey/Getty)

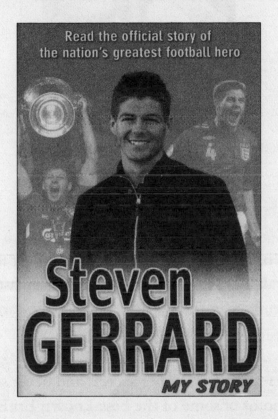

What does an Olympic champion eat for breakfast? How can you become the fastest runner in the world? At what age can you start training to be a boxer?

Interesting facts, super secrets and never seen photos of some of the best-known British sporting heroes, including boxer **Amir Khan**, runners **Mo Farah** and **Christine Ohuruogu**, basketball sensation **Luol Deng** and the gymnast **Louis Smith**.

**How did Bear Grylls become one
of the world's toughest adventurers?**

Known and admired by millions, Bear Grylls
has survived in dangerous environments few
would dare to visit. Find out what it's like
to take on mountaineering, martial arts,
parachuting, life in the SAS – and all
that nature can throw at you!

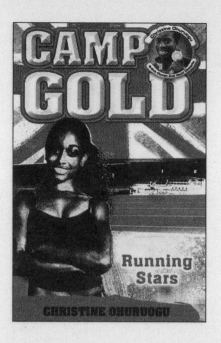

Maxine is crazy about sports! She's thrilled
to be going to Camp Gold, an elite sports
summer camp. She's nervous too —
will she be good enough?

Soon she's training for the Nationals, which
will be watched by Olympic champions. It's
tough but it'll be worth it if she wins. Then the
pranks start and her things go missing . . .
Someone is out to sabotage her chance
of winning. Can she stop them
before it's too late?

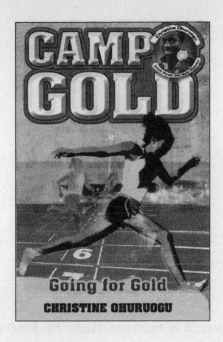

The minute Maxine arrives at Camp Gold
International, things start going wrong – her
training isn't going well and, worse, someone
has been vandalizing the plush building. Now
fingers are pointing at Maxine and her friends.

When it happens again, the principal makes
it clear that if the vandals don't stop, the camp
may be forced to close. For Maxine, Camp
Gold means everything. Can she solve
the mystery and focus on training
. . . and win?

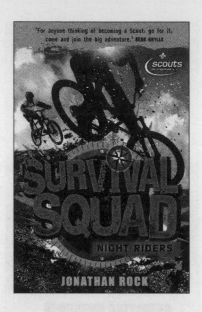

'For anyone thinking of becoming a Scout, go for it, come and join the big adventure.' BEAR GRYLLS

scouts

SURVIVAL SQUAD

NIGHT RIDERS

JONATHAN ROCK

There's a reason they're known as the Survival Squad . . .

An ordinary expedition for Tiger Patrol turns into an exciting adventure that involves paragliding, cycle racing and catching thieves in the night.

No matter what situation they're thrown into, they manage to come out on top . . . is there anything that Tiger Patrol can't do?

'For anyone thinking of becoming a Scout, go for it, come and join the big adventure.' BEAR GRYLLS

scouts

SURVIVAL SQUAD

WHITE WATER

JONATHAN ROCK

**There's a reason they're known
as the Survival Squad . . .**

Tiger Patrol's white-water expedition takes a
turn for the worse when the water level rises.
It's a matter of life or death, and they have
only their training and skill to rely on.

The first in an exciting series for children from
ex-SAS officer and bestselling adult author
Chris Ryan. Five kids, Alex, Li, Paulo, Hex
and Amber, are marooned on a desert island
where they must face the ultimate test –
survival! Killer komodo dragons, sharks and
modern day pirates are amongst the dangers
they face. Can the five bond as a
team – and stay alive?